Samuel Rutherford

SAMUEL RUTHERFORD (1600–1661)

"The King in His Beauty":
The Piety of Samuel Rutherford

Introduced and Edited by
Matthew Vogan

Reformation Heritage Books
Grand Rapids, Michigan

"The King in His Beauty"
© 2011 by Matthew Vogan

Published by
Reformation Heritage Books
2965 Leonard St. NE
Grand Rapids, MI 49525
616-977-0889/Fax: 616-285-3246
e-mail: orders@heritagebooks.org
website: www.heritagebooks.org

Printed in the United States of America
11 12 13 14 15 16/10 9 8 7 6 5 4 3 2 1

Rutherford, Samuel, 1600?-1661.
   "The King in His beauty" : the piety of Samuel Rutherford / introduced and edited by Matthew Vogan.
      p. cm. — (Profiles in Reformed spirituality)
   Includes bibliographical references (p.   ).
   ISBN 978-1-60178-125-3
   1. Christian life—Presbyterian authors. I. Vogan, Matthew. II. Title. III. Series.
   BV4501.3.R89 2011
   248.4'85—dc22
                                    2011005063

For additional Reformed literature, both new and used, request a free book list from Reformation Heritage Books at the above address.

For Janet

PSALM 90:14–17

PROFILES IN REFORMED SPIRITUALITY
series editors—Joel R. Beeke and Michael A. G. Haykin

Table of Contents

Profiles in Reformed Spirituality

Charles Dickens's famous line in *A Tale of Two Cities*—
"It was the best of times, it was the worst of times"
—seems well suited to western evangelicalism since
the 1960s. On the one hand, these decades have seen
much for which to praise God and to rejoice. In His
goodness and grace, for instance, Reformed truth is
no longer a house under siege. Growing numbers
identify themselves theologically with what we hold
to be biblical truth, namely, Reformed theology and
piety. And yet, as an increasing number of Reformed
authors have noted, there are many sectors of the
surrounding western evangelicalism that are charac-
terized by great shallowness and a trivialization of the
weighty things of God. So much of evangelical worship seems barren. And when it comes to spirituality,
there is little evidence of the riches of our heritage as
Reformed evangelicals.

As it was at the time of the Reformation, when the
watchword was *ad fontes*—"back to the sources"—so
it is now: The way forward is backward. We need to
go back to the spiritual heritage of Reformed evangelicalism to find the pathway forward. We cannot live
in the past; to attempt to do so would be antiquarian-
ism. But our Reformed forebearers in the faith can
teach us much about Christianity, its doctrines, its
passions, and its fruit.

And they can serve as our role models. As R. C. Sproul has noted of such giants as Augustine, Martin Luther, John Calvin, and Jonathan Edwards: "These men all were conquered, overwhelmed, and spiritually intoxicated by their vision of the holiness of God. Their minds and imaginations were captured by the majesty of God the Father. Each of them possessed a profound affection for the sweetness and excellence of Christ. There was in each of them a singular and unswerving loyalty to Christ that spoke of a citizenship in heaven that was always more precious to them than the applause of men."[1]

To be sure, we would not dream of placing these men and their writings alongside the Word of God. John Jewel (1522–1571), the Anglican apologist, once stated: "What say we of the fathers, Augustine, Ambrose, Jerome, Cyprian?... They were learned men, and learned fathers; the instruments of the mercy of God, and vessels full of grace. We despise them not, we read them, we reverence them, and give thanks unto God for them. Yet...we may not make them the foundation and warrant of our conscience: we may not put our trust in them. Our trust is in the name of the Lord."[2]

Seeking, then, both to honor the past and yet not idolize it, we are issuing these books in the series Profiles in Reformed Spirituality. The design is to introduce the spirituality and piety of the Reformed

---

1. R. C. Sproul, "An Invaluable Heritage," *Tabletalk* 23, no. 10 (October 1999): 5–6.

2. Cited in Barrington R. White, "Why Bother with History?" *Baptist History and Heritage* 4, no. 2 (July 1969): 85.

tradition by presenting descriptions of the lives of notable Christians with select passages from their works. This combination of biographical sketches and collected portions from primary sources gives a taste of the subjects' contributions to our spiritual heritage and some direction as to how the reader can find further edification through their works. It is the hope of the publishers that this series will provide riches for those areas where we are poor and light of day where we are stumbling in the deepening twilight.

—Joel R. Beeke
Michael A. G. Haykin

Abbreviations of Works by
Samuel Rutherford

Christ Dying — *Christ Dying, and Drawing Sinners to Himself* (London, 1647).

Communion Sermons — *Communion Sermons,* ed. A. A. Bonar (Edinburgh, 1876).

Covenant of Life — *The Covenant of Life Opened* (Edinburgh, 1655).

Free Disputation — *A Free Disputation against Pretended Liberty of Conscience* (London, 1649).

Influences — *The Influences of the Life of Grace* (London: Printed by T. C. for Andrew Crook, 1659).

Letters — *Letters of Samuel Rutherford* (1891; repr. Edinburgh: Banner of Truth, 1984).

Power and Prevalency — *The Power and Prevalency of Faith and Prayer evidenced in a practical discourse upon Matt. 9:27–31* (1713; repr. Stornoway: Reformation Press, 1991).

Quaint Sermons — *Quaint Sermons of Samuel Rutherford* (London: Hodder and Stoughton, 1885).

Catechism — *Rutherford's Catechism: Or, the Sum of the Christian Religion* (Edinburgh: Blue Banner Productions, 1988).

xiv   "The King in His Beauty"

Preface

Concerning Rutherford's writings, James Walker observes that "all will admit there is something about them *sui generis.*"[1] Initially, I was encouraged to read some of his treatises such as *Christ Dying and Drawing Sinners to Himself* by the enthusiasm of fellow academics at the University of Stirling who were entranced by his inimitable prose. Andrew Bonar refers to "the sparks of a fancy that sought to appropriate everything to spiritual purposes."[2] Rutherford moves easily between homely comparisons and Scholastic references, all of which need some explanation for the modern reader. It is commonly agreed that Rutherford is not only a uniquely powerful writer with a style marked by "tropical luxuriance" but also a writer with especially unique vocabulary and phraseology.[3] Many of the words that Rutherford uses are also now unfamiliar even to those who are well acquainted with the Scots language as it is now spoken. The language of the selections in this volume that have been drawn from Rutherford's writ-

---

1. James Walker, *Theology and Theologians of Scotland 1560–1750* (2nd ed., 1888; repr., Edinburgh, 1982), 8. The term *sui generis* means "of its own kind," that is, with characteristics unique to itself.

2. Andrew Bonar, "Sketch of Samuel Rutherford," in *Letters of Samuel Rutherford*, ed. Andrew Bonar (Edinburgh, 1891), 24.

3. Alexander Smellie, *Men of the Covenant* (Edinburgh: Banner of Truth, 1975), 67.

ings has also been updated a little in order to make it more accessible for the general reader. I am indebted in this to the painstaking assistance of Annette Gysen of Reformation Heritage Books. My hope is that this type of presentation will encourage many to attempt the less-traveled paths of the other spiritually rich writings of the "little, fair man" of whom the English merchant, having heard him preach, could say that he "showed me the loveliness of Christ."

—Matthew Vogan
Inverness
November 2010

Note of interest: The image used at the end of most selections is an illustration of St. Mary's College, St. Andrews, where Rutherford served as a professor of theology from 1639 until the end of his life.

Thine eyes shall see the king in his beauty: they shall behold the land that is very far off.

—Isaiah 33:17

I think that I see more of Christ than ever I saw; and yet I see but little of what may be seen. Oh that He would draw by the curtains, and that the King would come out of His gallery and His palace, that I might see Him!... Oh, what price can be given for Him. Angels cannot weigh Him. Oh, His weight, His worth, His sweetness, His overpassing beauty! If men and angels would come and look to that great and princely One, their ebbness [shallowness] could never take up His depth, their narrowness could never comprehend His breadth, height, and length. If ten thousand thousand worlds of angels were created, they might all tire themselves in wondering at His beauty, and begin again to wonder of new. Oh that I could win nigh Him, to kiss His feet, to hear His voice, to feel the smell of His ointments! But oh, alas! I have little, little of Him. Yet I long for more.

—Samuel Rutherford
Letters, no. 175, 331

Samuel Rutherford

Samuel Rutherford (1600–1661) and Christian Experience

Evangelicals have long recognized the unique character of Samuel Rutherford's *Letters,* ensuring their perennial popularity. Rutherford's contemporary, Richard Baxter, remarked that, excepting the Scriptures, the world had never seen a book quite like Rutherford's *Letters.* C. H. Spurgeon had the highest of praise: "When we are dead and gone," he wrote, "let the world know that Spurgeon held Rutherford's letters to be the nearest thing to inspiration which can be found in all the writings of mere men."[1] Principal John Macleod reckoned them "the most remarkable series of devotional letters that the literature of the Reformed Churches can show."[2]

Robert McWard, Rutherford's close colleague, first edited the *Letters.* In the original preface, McWard comments on Rutherford: "If thou wilt but converse with him a little, it may be thou find thy heart burn within thee while thou talkest with this warm soul, whose words seem, as they drop, to cast fire into

---

1. As quoted in John Coffey, *Politics, Religion, and the British Revolutions* (Cambridge: Cambridge University Press, 1997), 6.

2. John Macleod, *Scottish Theology in Relation to Church History since the Reformation* (Edinburgh: Banner of Truth, 1974), 68.

the affections, and set the heart in a flame."[3] A later editor of some of Rutherford's sermons commented, "His style is savoury to a spiritual taste, and also moving. As he was pious and devout, without affectation, he had a particular talent of handling divine things so as to fix the attentions and affect the heart. This *gustus pietatis* [taste of piety] that is so discernible in his writings, and for which he was so famous, is a clear evidence of a rich stock of grace and a large unction from the Holy One."[4]

Rutherford's other works are not as widely known as his letters, yet many of them have the same intense devotional character and spiritual power. This brief volume seeks to summarize the distinctive insight into Christian experience witnessed in Rutherford's writings and to introduce their devotional qualities. Rutherford's spirit is well summed up in some of his own words:

> Strive to make prayer and reading and holy company and holy conference your delight; and when delight comes in, you shall by little and little smell the sweetness of Christ, till at length your soul be over head and ears in Christ's sweetness. Then shall you be taken up to the top of the mountain with the Lord, to know the ravishments of spiritual love, and the glory and excellency of a seen, revealed, felt, and embraced Christ; and then you shall not be able to loose yourself off Christ, and to bind your soul to old lovers.[5]

---

3. Preface, *Letters of Samuel Rutherford*, ed. A. A. Bonar (Edinburgh: Oliphant, Anderson, and Ferrier, 1891), 725.

4. *Power and Prevalency*, xi–xii.

5. *Letters*, no. 199, 391.

The Necessity of Christian Experience

Samuel Rutherford was born around the year 1600 in Nisbet, a small village in the Scottish Borders. Rutherford later reflected that it was a place where "Christ was scarce named, as touching any reality or power of godliness."[6] Some of Rutherford's remarks in his letters indicate that his conversion most likely took place at university in Edinburgh when he was well into his twenties. He laments not having followed Christ much earlier. In a letter to Robert Stuart he writes, "Ye have gotten a great advantage in the way of heaven, that ye have started to the gate in the morning. Like a fool, as I was, I suffered my sun to be high in the heaven, and near afternoon, before I ever took the gate by the end."[7]

It is likely, however, that his first experience of Christ was a powerful one when we consider his words: "At the Lord's first meeting with a sinner, the Lord opens his heart by grace to let Him in, and there they sup together. There is a feast of love between them." Also, "No man can love Christ till He love him first, because our love of Christ is nothing else but an effect of this love to us…. So we may learn to sing for ever a song of free grace shown in our conversion."[8] Rutherford explains this further in another sermon: "When sinners have been going on into a course of rebellion, running away from God, after their humiliation ordinarily He fills them with a feast of the sense of His love, all their days they

---

6. Ibid., no. 345, 680.

7. Ibid., no. 186, 364.

8. *Quaint Sermons*, 251, 252.

Rutherford first attended a school that was housed in the
ancient Jedburgh Abbey, a few miles from his home.

Photo courtesy of Douglas Bond.

cannot forget." God begins His work of grace by shattering the "towers of pride, of worldly-mindedness, of filthiness," but then overwhelms the sinner with His presence and His beauty.[9]

Believing that "faith...worketh by love" (Gal. 5:6), Rutherford emphasizes the centrality of the affections in the soul, which are

> like the needle, the rest of the soul like the thread; and as the needle makes way and draws the thread, so holy affections pull forward and draw all to Jesus. The affections are the lower part of the soul, and when they are filled they set all the soul on work; when there is any love in the affections, it sets all the rest of the faculties of the soul on work to duty, and when there is any corruption in the affections, it stagnates the soul, will, mind, and conscience. Affections are the feet of the soul, and the wheels whereupon the conscience runs. When a man is off his feet he cannot run or walk; so when the affections are lame, the soul moves on crutches.[10]

Rutherford compares the sinner in conversion to a fish hooked by the angler. The affections are moved, and faith works by these affections. Perhaps there was much of his first experience of grace in this description:

> As when a fish is taken there are two actions, the bait alluring and beguiling the fish with hope of meat. This is like the working of the word which is Christ's bait; but when He wins us to dry land, then, when the fish is hooked, there is a real

---

9. Ibid., 353, 339.

10. *Communion Sermons*, 316.

action of the fisher, drawing and hauling the fish to land; it leapeth and flightering [fluttering] and wrestling while it bleeds with the hook. And this answereth to the Holy Spirit's powerful hauling and drawing of the soul in all the affections, that the soul feeleth joy, comfort, delight, desire, longing, believing, nibbling and biting Christ's bait.[11]

For Rutherford, true religion involves spiritual experience just as much as belief in right doctrine and holy obedience to the Word of God. Life's goal is to enjoy God as well as to glorify Him. Rutherford would have agreed with his pupil, the Covenanter Robert Fleming (son of the minister James Fleming, with whom Rutherford corresponded), on the subject of Christian experience. Fleming writes,

Oh what an empty thing religion should be if it had not this word experience in its grammar; that secret and sure mark whereby the Christian knoweth the scripture is of God; how thus the Lord hath sealed their instruction in a dark plunge; how life and power, enlivening influences, to the melting of their heart have oft trysted them in a very dead frame and now they know that verily God heareth prayer; now they are persuaded and have learned by the cross that he is indeed a comforter."[12]

Some professing Christians seem to avoid experience in the Christian life and are reluctant to be too "all out" for Christ. The type of person that cannot

---

11. *Quaint Sermons*, 92–93.

12. Robert Fleming, *The Fulfilling of the Scripture* (1669; repr., Edinburgh, 1845), I:10.

"bide heat and forwardness in religion" complains: "I love Christ...but I would not make a blowing horn of my religion. They shall never know upon what side I am."[13] This half-hearted man is afraid that too much zeal in Christian things will affect his material prosperity and status in this world, but the Scriptures tell us, "It is good to be zealously affected always in a good thing" (Gal. 4:18). In his letters Rutherford continually urges the necessity of giving diligence to make our personal calling and election sure: "Heaven is not at the next door. I find Christianity to be a hard task.... We would all keep both Christ and our right eye, our right hand and foot; but it will not do with us."[14] "God detesteth lukewarmness, and coldness in His matters and demands 'all the heart, all the soul, all the strength' of His people (Deut. 6:5). [Even] if you had ten tongues to speak for God, a hundred hands to fight for Him, many lives to lose for Him, Ahithophel's wisdom to employ in His services, except you engage the heart and affections in His service, you do nothing to Him" (1 Cor. 13).[15]

The temptation of an insincere appeal to Christ is powerful; we are all too comfortable in Zion, enthusiastic to be saved and happy but not so much to be saved and holy. "Oh, how many of us would have Christ divided into two halves, that we might take the half of Him only! We take His office, Jesus, and Salvation: but 'Lord' is a cumbersome word, and to obey and work out our own salvation, and to perfect

---

13. *Quaint Sermons*, 136–37.

14. *Letters*, no. 124, 249.

15. *Sermon Preached...Commons* (Edinburgh, 1644), 17, 23.

holiness, is the cumbersome and stormy northside of Christ that we eschew and shift [avoid]."[16]

Prayer and Christian Experience

Samuel Rutherford began his ministry in Anwoth, Kirkcudbrightshire, during 1627, being ordained in the Presbyterian way, which did not require him to give any acknowledgment to the bishop. Prayer was key to Rutherford's ministry in Anwoth. Those who knew him said that he seemed "to be always praying, always preaching, always visiting the sick, always catechizing, always writing and studying."[17] Rutherford and his contemporaries seem to have been especially eminent in prayer.[18] Bonar says that Rutherford was a man so enraptured with Christ that he "was known to fall asleep at night talking of Christ, and even to speak of Him during his sleep."[19] Rutherford himself wrote that "even to dream of Him is sweet."[20] Arising at three o'clock each morning in order to pray, he was in constant, earnest intercession for his flock. "There I wrestled with the Angel and prevailed," he says. "Wood, trees, meadows and hills are my witnesses, that I drew on a fair meeting

---

16. *Letters*, no. 234, 467.

17. Samuel Rutherford, *Letters* (1905), 5.

18. This is quite evident from the fact that on fast-day services one of the Westminster divines would be called upon to pray for an hour at a time. See *Minutes of the Sessions of the Westminster Assembly of Divines*, eds. A. F. Mitchell and J. Struthers (Edinburgh: W. Blackwood and Sons, 1874).

19. *Letters*, 5.

20. Ibid., no. 277, 537.

betwixt Christ and [the congregation at] Anwoth."[21]
Also, at Anwoth he made a covenant with young
George Gillespie that each would pray for the other
throughout the rest of their days.[22]

Besides his letters, so full of spiritual prayer
for fellow believers, the lost, the church, and the
in-gathering of the Jews, Rutherford wrote various
books that are extremely helpful for understanding prayer. *The Trial and Triumph of Faith* considers
the patient, humble, and persevering prayers of the
Syro-Phoenician woman in her entreaties to Christ.
The Power of Faith and Prayer is a set of sermons on
the two blind men in Matthew 9:27–31 who follow
Christ, crying out to Him for mercy. *The Influences of
the Life of Grace* is a practical treatise that deals with
the vital theme of our need for the gracious influences of the Holy Spirit upon us and prayer as an
all-important means to this end.

Prayer must be in faith. As Rutherford puts it,
"Praying without faith is breathing of wind, and
sounds without life.... But praying with faith is like
the breathings of a living man, that is hot and nour-
ishes life, and keeps the body in a vital heat of life as
long as it continues in the body."[23] Before we pray,
we should also consider the state and frame of our
heart and prepare it; otherwise, our prayer will be the
sacrifice of fools. It is impossible to pray acceptably in
anger, deceitfulness, worldly mindedness, or pride.[24]

---

21. Ibid., no. 279, 540–41.
22. Cf. ibid., no. 144, 275.
23. *Power and Prevalency*, 24.
24. *Influences*, 421–22.

We must pray in order to pray rather than rush head-long into duties. "Prayer is like God's file to stir a rusty heart."[25] There are, of course, exceptions to this, such as ejaculatory prayers or emergency cries that we must simply send to heaven impulsively rather than prepare ourselves; but ordinarily there should be preparation.[26]

The Spirit of adoption is the Spirit of prayer, making us cry, "Abba, Father." Earthly children, "because they are sons, seek all things they need from their father."[27] In his catechism Rutherford asks, "How shall we know that we are adopted?" The practical response follows: "If we can pray to our Father; if we be in fashion like our Father and our brother Christ, serving for the inheritance as heirs, not for the moveables as slaves."[28]

"No music delights [God] more [than] the sighs and tears, complaints and prayers of his children."[29] Rutherford emphasized that vehemence and crying in prayer are both necessary and natural. Hunger and necessity cannot afford to be modest and under-stated. "An arrow drawn with full strength hath a speedier flight; therefore, the prayers of the saints are expressed by crying in Scripture." Christ prayed with "strong crying and tears" or "war-shouts…. The cry addeth wings to the prayer." It is effectual—"This poor man cried, and the LORD heard him, and saved

---

25. *Quaint Sermons*, 134.

26. *Influences*, 312.

27. *Catechism*, 64.

28. Ibid., 63.

29. *Communion Sermons*, 259.

him out of all his troubles" (Ps. 34:6). Vehement prayer is importunate. James 5:16 asserts that prayer is fervent as well as effectual, and this word *fervent*, as Rutherford explains, literally intimates "prayer possessed with...fervour of spirit."[30] Fervent, vehement prayer is called "wrestling, as Jacob by prayer wrestled with God. Now, in wrestling, the whole man is employed and all his strength, all the bones, nerves, legs and arms of the soul are set to work in praying."[31] Jacob had a princely power over the angel and prevailed; he wept and made supplication to Him.

Rutherford deals with practical difficulties that believers may face in their prayer struggles. Even broken prayers are heard: "Every broken parcel of prayer is prayer," he counsels. To those who lament "I find I cannot speak at all," he notes that even groaning, tears, or just a look are all classified as prayer in Scripture (Pss. 6:8; 69:3; 102:20; Isa. 38:14). "Words are but the body, the garment, the outside of prayer; sighs are nearer the heart-work."[32] What about when we are not answered in our prayers? This is perhaps the most difficult aspect of prayer to deal with. Why does prayer seem to be unanswered? How do we know when we are answered? In respect to the first question, Rutherford responds that the delay in answers to prayer has a merciful and beneficial aspect to it. "Christ often heareth when He doth not answer; His not answering is an answer, and speaks thus, Pray on, go on, and cry; for the Lord holdeth

---

30. *Trial and Triumph*, 66–67.

31. *Power and Prevalency*, 39.

32. Ibid., 68–73.

His door fast bolted, not to keep out, but that you may knock and knock. Patience to wait for the answer is itself an answer. Prayer is to God, worship; to us, often, it is but a servant upon mere necessity sent on a business."[33] Even prayers that would seem to be lost and wasted are not so at all; they are both heard and answered. Rutherford explains:

> I may pray for victory to God's people in a battle; they lose, yet I am heard and answered because I prayed for that victory not under the notion of victory, but as linked with mercy to the church and the honor of Christ. The formal object of my prayers was a spiritual mercy to the church and the honor of Jesus Christ. The Lord hath shown mercy to His people by humbling them and glorifies His Son in preserving a fallen people. He hears what is spiritual and not the errors.[34]

We are heard when we ask in faith according to God's will. How shall we know we are answered? Hannah knew because of peace after prayer. Paul knew by receiving new supply to bear the want of what he sought in prayer. Liberty and boldness of faith are other indications.

Conscience and Christian Experience

Rutherford's ministry in Anwoth was not to continue unmolested, however. He had conscientiously avoided acknowledging the bishop at his ordination, and now he spoke out publicly against the Arminian doctrine that the bishops were seeking to popular-

---

33. Ibid., 115.
34. Ibid., 117.

ANWOTH OLD KIRK
SAMUEL RUTHERFORD
MINISTER FROM 1627 - 1638

PROFESSOR OF DIVINITY AND PRINCIPAL OF ST MARY'S COLLEGE, 1647-1661.
BURIED IN THE CATHEDRAL GROUNDS, ST ANDREWS, 1661.

COUNSELLOR IN THE WESTMINSTER ASSEMBLY OF DIVINES.
AUTHOR OF FAMOUS "LETTERS" AND "LEX REX".
PREACHER OF PERMANENT RENOWN.
REFORMER AND DEFENDER OF THE FAITH.

MONUMENT ERECTED TO HIS MEMORY ON THE NEAR-BY HILL, 1842.

'FAIR ANWOTH BY THE SOLWAY'
'GLORY, GLORY DWELLETH IN EMMANUEL'S LAND'

The church in Anwoth where Rutherford
began his pastorate in 1627.

Photos courtesy of Mark Landon.

ize. His first publication, *Exercitationes Apologeticae pro Divina Gratia,* which opposed the Arminian error that had become such a close ally of episcopacy and semi-Roman Catholic ceremonialism, led to his being tried before the High Commission in 1636. It was for publishing this treatise, for failing to recognize the authority of the High Commission and not giving the bishops their titles, such as "lord," that he was deposed and exiled to Aberdeen.

Rutherford was content to suffer for the cause of Christ. Like Robert Bruce before him, who also had been punished with banishment, he always maintained the vital importance of the conscience. It was, he believed, "the principal part of [the] soul.... The judging part of the soul under God, teaching and counseling good and comforting us when we do it... and forbidding ill and tormenting us after we have committed ill."[35] Rutherford argued that the conscience is "something of God, a domestic little God, a keeper sent from heaven."[36] He emphasized our solemn responsibility in relation to our conscience: "Seeing we carry our judge with us in our breast which we take either to heaven or hell with us, and cannot put on or off our conscience as we do our garments, we should fear to sin before our conscience."[37]

An individual's conscience should not therefore merely "lie beside him as the wretch's Gold, which for many years seeth neither sun nor wind; but it is a

---

35. *Catechism*, 16.

36. *Free Disputation*, 9.

37. *Catechism*, 18.

Conscience walking in the streets, and in action."[38] It should be active, but it should not always be trusted. Since conscience can be mistaken for fancy, novelty, or heresy, it must be informed by and in subjection to the Word of God: "The more of knowledge, the more of conscience, as the more of fire, the more heat."[39] Again, Rutherford emphasizes the authority of God's Word: "The Word of God must be the rule of conscience, and conscience is a servant, and an under-judge only, not a Lord."[40]

Conscience, therefore, should be tender and sensitive. "It cannot be denied but the more tenderness, the more of God, and the more of conscience; but by tenderness is meant fear and awesomeness of sin."[41] He once wrote to his congregation, exhorting them: "Hold fast what ye have received. Keep the truth once delivered. If ye or that people quit it in a hair, or in a hoof, ye break your conscience in twain; and who then can mend it, and cast a knot on it?"[42] Like the apostle Paul, Rutherford could say, "And herein do I exercise myself, to have always a conscience void to offence toward God, and toward men" (Acts 24:16).

The Heights of Christian Experience
It is to this period of exile in Aberdeen that we owe over 220 of Rutherford's 365 letters. Here, in his iso-

38. *Free Disputation*, 1.

39. Ibid., 5.

40. Ibid., 10.

41. Ibid., 19.

42. *Letters*, no. 180, 347.

lation, Rutherford trysted with the Lord Jesus Christ in especially deep soul communion. "I find that my extremity hath sharpened the edge of His love and kindness, as that He seemeth to devise new ways of expressing the sweetness of His love to my soul."[43] In his letters we find that he overflows in speaking of Christ. He expresses this necessity of glorifying Christ in a letter to Viscount Kenmure: "I must tell you what lovely Jesus, fair Jesus, King Jesus hath done to my soul."[44] In Aberdeen, Rutherford rejoiced in a spring-time of spiritual experience, and he could say, "Lo, the winter is past" (Song 2:11). He describes these heights of spiritual experience: "The believer hath flowings of strong acts of faith, joy, love; supernatural passions of grace arising to a high spring-tide, above the banks and ordinary coasts."[45]

At such times Christ brings His beloved into His banqueting house, where they are "feasted with love banquets."[46] Although such feasts are not the portion of all saints at all times, none of Christ's people are ever restricted: "He alloweth feasts to all the bairns [children] within God's household."[47] The joy to be anticipated in Communion seasons belongs to the faithful who discern them as feasts, "wherein our Well-Beloved Jesus rejoiceth and is merry with His friends."[48] As Rutherford puts it, using the language

---

43. Ibid., no. 179, 341.
44. Ibid., no. 177, 336.
45. *Christ Dying*, 27–28.
46. *Letters*, no. 69, 148.
47. Ibid., no. 179, 342.
48. Ibid., no. 14, 58.

of the Song of Solomon, "There is a time when [Christ] comes to His garden to feast upon the honeycomb and His spiced wine, and then the spouse has a rich feast of love and of the dainties of Heaven, and is taken in to the King's house of wine and Christ's banner over her is love (Song 2:4). 'And His left hand is under' her 'head, and his right hand doth embrace' her (Song 2:6)."[49]

Rutherford learned not to make too much of these experiences, however. He knew that he could not always expect these heights of spiritual experience, as he explains,

> As there are some highest manifestations of God, in which experience teaches us that the saints would not be able to keep the use of a tabernacle of clay with that little Heaven, so neither are the saints to make high manifestations God's constant rule. As David's soul is filled with marrow and fatness, he may desire the same again. "My soul thirsteth for thee...in a dry and thirsty land, where no water is; to see thy power and thy glory, so as I have seen thee in the sanctuary" (Ps. 63:1–2)....
> Again, let a believer have such a rapture as Paul had, when ravished to the third heaven, as the saints may have the like in another spiritual way, yet is he not to lay down this ground: "Sure I shall have as high a manifestation of God, ere I die, as this was." Are believers, when heightened above their ordinary in the visions of God here below, to conclude that they shall have as sweet and as high

---

49. *Power and Prevalency*, 61.

manifestations of God again? No, they are not, unless it were revealed that it shall be so.[50]

The Focus of Christian Experience

Like the psalmist, Rutherford could say, "Whom have I in heaven but thee? and there is none upon earth that I desire beside thee" (Ps. 73:25). "Let me have no joy but the warmness and fire of Christ's love; I seek no other, God knoweth. If this love be taken from me, the bottom is fallen out of all my happiness and joy."[51] He often said that heaven would be no heaven at all and he would be unwilling to go there if Christ Himself were not there.[52] The Christian's "affections leap out and embrace Christ about the neck."[53] There is an exclusive focus: "Nothing is fixedly sought after, but God, He only feared and served.... [He] only desired...the soul sick of love for only Christ."[54] Whereas our "duties to Prince, parents, husband, wife, children, [and] Parliament" require only "half" affections, God alone seeks the whole of our affections, such that with David, we seek "after the living God," longing, fainting, and crying out for Him.[55]

He encourages others to enjoy the same experience of Christ: "Brother, I may, from new experience, speak of Christ to you. Oh, if ye saw in Him what I

---

50. Ibid., 75.

51. *Letters*, no. 212, 415.

52. *Letters*, no. 104, 215.

53. *Communion Sermons*, 316.

54. Ibid., 38; *Covenant of Life*, 151.

55. *Sermon Preached...Commons*, 23.

see! A river of God's unseen joys has flowed from
bank to brae [above ordinary bounds] over my soul
since I parted with you. I wish that I wanted part,
so being ye might have; that your soul might be sick
of love for Christ, or rather satiated with Him."[56]
Rutherford counseled that much time must be given
in secret to cultivating communion with Christ. We
ought increasingly to value Christ in His person and
work. "Estimation produceth love, even the love of
Christ; and love is a great favorite, and is much at
court, and dwelleth constantly with the king. To be
much with Christ, especially in secret, late and early,
and to give much time to converse with Christ, spea-
keth much love; and the love of Christ is of the same
largeness and quantity with grace, for grace and love
keep proportion one with another."[57]

Rutherford's description of true love in exercise to
Christ probes our own experience acutely:

This speaks much soul-love to be where he is.
Cant. [Song] 1:7.... To be able to write a spiritual chronicle and history of all Christ's stirrings
towards your soul saith ye have letters daily, and
good intelligence of the affairs of the Spirit, and
of the King's Court, and that He writes to you,
as Cant. 5:1. "I am come into my garden, my
sister, my spouse; I have gathered my myrrh with
my spice, I have eaten my honey-comb with my
honey, I have drunk my wine with my milk": then
will Christ write a letter to spiritual ones, and (as
it were, with reverence to His holiness) give a

---

56. *Letters,* no. 147, 278.

57. *Trial and Triumph,* 265.

sort of account where He is, what He does, what thoughts He hath to us. O! how few know this?[58]

The ultimate emphasis of experience must always be upon Christ alone. Sometimes Rutherford corrects himself, as it were, to say that Christ is more to be extolled than His gifts: "I would not have Christ's love entering into me, but I would enter into it, and be swallowed up of that love. But I see not myself here; for I fear I make more of His love than of Himself; whereas Himself is far beyond and much better than His love."[59] Rutherford believed passionately that life is to be lived with Christ preeminent in everything. "For to me to live is Christ" (Phil. 1:21) was the motto written over all of his life. His life was so much intertwined with the Lord Jesus that he could speak concerning a trial that "Christ and I will bear it."[60] The most glorious and simplest truth that he knew was, "my Christ is God," and having made this humble but intimate confession he says, "I have said all things, I can say no more. I would that I could build as much on this, 'My Christ is God,' as it would bear. I might lay all the world upon it."[61]

Rutherford loved to trace Christ's love for him back to eternity and the covenant made with the Father:

Was His consent to the Covenant but as late and young as since Adam fell or Abraham was called to leave his country and his father's house (Gen. 3; 12)? Ah! It's an older love than so: A yester-

---

58. *Covenant of Life*, 142.

59. *Letters*, no. 178, 339.

60. Ibid., no. 69, 149.

61. Ibid., no. 178, 338.

day's love, time-mercy, a grace of the age with the world could not have saved me. Nor were our Charters and Writs of Gospel-grace first drawn up in Paradise. Nay, but copies and doubles of them only were given to Adam in Paradise. The love of God is no younger than God and was never younger to sinners.... I desire to hold me fast by that: "I have loved thee with an everlasting love" (Jer. 31:3).[62]

The Depths of Christian Experience

Grace has its winter as well as its springtime or summer, and the felt presence of Christ easily gives way to keenly felt absence.[63] The floods of the high springtide quickly drain away: "Often the time of some extreme desertion and soul-trouble is, when Christ hath been in the soul with a full, high spring tide of divine manifestations of Himself."[64] This is the nature of Christian experience according to Rutherford. "The condition in ebbings and flowings, in full manifestations and divine raptures of another world, when the wind bloweth right from heaven, and the breath of Jesus Christ's mouth, and of sad absence, runneth through the Song of Solomon, the book of Psalms, the book of Job."[65]

Even this absence can be fruitful, however, since it encourages longing for Christ's return: "Sick nights for the Lord's absence in not drawing are most spiri-

---

62. *Covenant of Life*, 307–308.

63. *Power and Prevalency*, 61.

64. *Christ Dying*, 50.

65. Ibid., 27–28.

tual signs."[66] This withdrawing is good for our growth and for quickening our desires for Him: "As night and shadows are good for flowers, and moonlight and dews are better than a continual sun, so is Christ's absence of special use…. It hath some nourishing virtue in it, and giveth sap to humility." When Christ is absent, our obedience is "quicker and more powerful" than it is "under feeling and presence."[67] "Patient submission to God under desertion is sweet."[68] Rutherford counsels that when our consciences undergo a deep sense of sin and we sense the absence of God's favor, "we should not give sleep to our eyes [until] we confess and repent, and should seek to the covenant and mercy of God who cannot forget us."[69] He is conscious that this is not always attainable, however, for the weak and troubled believer. "Then, like a man in a dark house who cannot see either door or window, but [gropes] to the door with his hands, we should deem well of God, still believe and run to old experience both in ourselves and others."[70]

When we seek Christ above all, we are even able to say, "I love Christ's worst reproaches, His glooms, His cross, better than all the world's plastered glory."[71] We must remember that we are not yet in heaven: "There are no desertions in heaven, no hiding of God's face, no cloud, no night, no change, nothing but a sun in its

---

66. Ibid., 261.

67. *Quaint Sermons*, 98.

68. *Trial and Triumph*, 156.

69. *Catechism*, 71.

70. Ibid.

71. *Letters*, no. 105, 218.

full strength; always day without night, a full sunshine without a cloud or a shadow. Grace in us is a habit, and not always in action, and our stability here (as touching the other) is Hebrews 13:14: 'That we have no continuing city here, but we seek one to come.'"[72]

The Sovereignty of God in Christian Experience

These depths are to be explained by God's sovereignty and the providences of His will in apportioning our spiritual experience according to the wisdom of His intimate knowledge of us. There are often times when the "causes of His withdrawings are unknown to us," because, quite simply, "ways of high sovereignty and dominion of grace are far out of the sight of angels and men." "His comforts and His answers are His own free graces; He may do with His own what He thinks good, and grace is no debt. 'Hear, O Lord, for Thy own sake' (Dan. 9:19)."[73] In many cases God's withdrawing will be a result of sin that hinders communion. It is not always, however, simply the case that we are not seeking the blessing to our utmost. "Christ walks in a path of unsearchable liberty.... Some are in the suburbs of heaven, and feel the dainties of the King's higher house, ere they are in heaven; and others, children of the same Father, passengers on the same journey, wade through hell, darkness of fears, thorns of doubtings, and have few love-tokens till the marriage day."[74] Our duty is to submit and to persevere in prayer: "If we could but

---

72. *Sermon Preached...Commons*, 14–15.

73. *Letters*, no. 342, 675; *Trial and Triumph*, 156.

74. *Christ Dying*, 49–50.

weep upon Him, and in the holy pertinacity of faith wrestle with Him, and say, 'We will not let Thee go,' it may be that then, He, who is easy to be entreated, would yet, notwithstanding of our high provocations, condescend to stay and feed among the lilies."[75]

Rutherford wrote *The Influences of the Life of Grace* in order to deal with the question of how divine sovereignty and human responsibility work together in the matter of spiritual growth and experience. It is a neglected theme, although intensely practical for the Christian every day in his devotional life.[76] The interrelation of divine sovereignty and human responsibility is a difficult area of doctrine, and Rutherford seeks to expound various portions of Scripture in exploring the issue. On the text Philippians 2:12–13— "Work out your own salvation with fear and trembling. For it is God which worketh in you both to will and to do of his good pleasure"—Rutherford comments,

> How the connection is between our working and the effectual predeterminating influences of God, is to us dark, but this argument of Paul saith they well agree, and he infers this thesis, they both physically and morally are to work out their salvation, in whom God both by the habit and actual influences of grace worketh to will and to do, then must influences of grace so be at hand when the believers are to act, as they are no less under a precept, and a command to act, believe, pray, than

---

75. *Letters*, no. 28, 88.

76. *Influences*, A.

the husband-man is under a command to plow in summer, and to sow, lest he be poor.'[77]

Rutherford shows that the same connection between divine sovereignty and God's creation is seen in His work of providence:

Influences are acts of God concurring with cre-ated causes under Him, and a sort of continued creation; as God of nothing makes all things, so in His providence He gives a day to all borrowed beings, in their being preserved by Him, and they are the Lord's debtors, in being acted by Him, or then they could not stir nor move."[78]

The Influences of the Life of Grace deals with the ques-tion of what believers should do when they do not feel spiritually exercised. Rutherford responds by showing that believers are to do their duty in prayer and wor-ship no matter how they feel. Sometimes Christians can fall into the error of thinking that they can never pray unless they are consciously moved by the Holy Spirit. This is wrong, Rutherford says, because the warrant of prayer is not the gracious influences that the Most High may or may not supply. Our moral duty is determined by the divine command. We must pray for the Spirit's help, but we must take care to make the Word our only rule, and not our feelings. How can the feelings of the Spirit be known but by the Word? If everything depended on our feelings, the Word would be useless. The command cries to the conscience; the voice of the Lord sounds in the

---

77. Ibid., 5.

78. Ibid., 1.

Word. Pray continually. "Call upon me in the day of trouble" (Ps. 50:15). We cannot excuse ourselves by supposing that the Spirit's influences are absent.

Like the farmer who cannot hold back from plowing and sowing because he does not find a time as desirable as he would like, we have a responsibility to pray, even though we may not feel moved by the Spirit: "He that observeth the wind shall not sow; and he that regardeth the clouds shall not reap" (Eccl. 11:4).[79] Rutherford emphasizes that we do not have dominion over the actions of the Spirit. God blows in this wind with greater sovereignty than in any natural wind.[80]

The Lord gives influences according to His will of pleasure (secret will), but we must stir and pray and act according to His will of command (revealed will). This is illustrated throughout Psalm 119 where both prayer and the need of the influences of grace are interwoven. In verse 25 the psalmist writes that God's influences have been withdrawn: "My soul cleaveth unto the dust." There immediately follows a petition: "Quicken thou me according to thy word." This shows how we should respond to the sovereign withdrawal of influences in the secret will of God. We take up the duty of praying according to His revealed will and pray for those very influences to be restored.[81]

God's sovereignty is mysterious in connection with prayer, especially a prayer for quickening. Ulti-

---

79. Ibid., 55, 64–65.

80. *Power and Prevalency*, 60.

81. *Influences*, 381.

mately, such a prayer in faith will be effectual in the experience of the believer. In the meantime, however, the Lord uses prayer to keep the soul under sufficient graces. It provides fresh showers, giving the burned man who patiently endures the fire refreshment, while cooling and expelling the heat. Rutherford says that suffering pain in faith and joy is more excellent than having the pain removed.[82]

The "Lord's way of coming to us, and our way of coming to Him" is through His appointed means.[83] The "influences of grace," which are necessary for an individual to persevere to the end in faith, are ordinarily conveyed through the use of means such as prayer, the Scriptures, and the sacraments. Although God has the sovereign liberty to bestow His influences according to His own secret will and purpose, He has promised them in His appointed means.[84] The believer must pray away spiritual indisposition. Spiritual dispositions ebb and flow in the diligent use of or neglect of these means.[85] What Rutherford speaks of as "spiritual heart-burnings" are spiritual dispositions that should be experienced in the diligent use of these means: "Heavenly heart-burning goes along with the Scriptures.... With the Scriptures so opened and applied by the spirit of Jesus as by a strong power, burning coals are cast into the heart."[86] The whole treatise is a rich contribution to understanding Christian experience in

---

82. Ibid., 408–409.

83. Ibid., 96.

84. Ibid., 96–97, 373–75.

85. Ibid., 301.

86. Ibid., 248.

a more biblical and systematic way, while retaining a practical emphasis for the individual believer.

Christian Experience and National Religion

Rutherford believed that grace in exercise would lead Christians to do as much as they can for the cause of Christ in this world: "The more gracious men are, the more public they are" since "he who is for the Bridegroom cannot be against the Bride."[87] For this reason, he saw that public and private duties are inextricably linked together, and his conviction of the sovereign and entire providence of God meant that there was a public significance to individual experience. The signing of the National Covenant at Edinburgh in 1638 was a powerfully personal as well as national act for many. Some signed their name using their own blood. It was publicly sworn with uplifted hands and many tears. As Robert Fleming observed, many could trace their conversion from that time. "Since the land was engaged by covenant to the Lord... what a solemn outletting of the Spirit hath been seen, a large harvest with much of the fruit of the Gospel discernible, which...hath been proved in the inbringing of thousands to Christ."[88]

As events developed, there was hope that the reformation and revival witnessed in Scotland would spread to the other parts of the British Isles. Rutherford therefore welcomed the opportunity, as one of the Scottish commissioners, to take part in the

---

87. *Sermon Preached...Commons*, 5–6.

88. As quoted in John Gillies, *Historical Collections of Accounts of Revival* (Edinburgh: Banner of Truth, 1981), 201.

The Westminster Abbey in London was the site of
the Westminster Assembly; Rutherford was one of the
Scottish commissioners invited to attend, and he
stayed longer than any of the others.

Westminster Assembly, which was convened to settle the doctrine, government, and worship of the British churches. He hoped to be instrumental in building "the waste places of Zion in another kingdom."[89] He took up his seat in the assembly in November 1643 and remained in London until November 1647. Here, he published five major books in defense of Presbyterian church government and in opposition to antinomian doctrine. One of the most prominent participants in the Assembly's debates on theology and church polity, he also preached twice before the Long Parliament, pleading with them to pursue reformation of the church in England and Ireland in uniformity with Scotland. In a sermon preached before the English Parliament in June 1644, he revealed his heart's longing for peace and unity based on true reformation: "Shall we kill and devour one another all day and lodge together in heaven at night and can we say to one another in heaven, 'Hast thou found me, O mine enemy?'…and yet on earth must we be at daggers, at rents, at divisions; are there two Christs because two nations?"[90]

Rutherford's perspective in relation to national religion was much the same as the Solemn League and Covenant sworn to by the British Isles in 1643. It began with the vow that "we shall sincerely, really, and constantly, through the grace of God, endeavor, in our several places and callings, the preservation of the reformed religion…[in order] that we, and our posterity after us, may, as brethren, live in faith and

---

89. *Letters*, no. 308, 615.

90. *Sermon Preached…Commons*, 5–6.

love, and the Lord may delight to dwell in the midst of us." It went on to abominate, with Rutherfordian passion, "detestable indifference or neutrality in this cause." At the conclusion of the Covenant there is a confession that

> we have not endeavored to receive Christ in our hearts, nor to walk worthy of Him in our lives; which are the causes of other sins and transgression so much abounding amongst us: and our true and unfeigned purpose, desire, and endeavor, for ourselves, and all others under our power and charge, both in public and private, in all duties we owe to GOD and man, to amend our lives, and each one to go before another in the example of a real reformation; that the Lord may turn away His wrath and heavy indignation, and establish these Churches and kingdoms in truth and peace.[91]

Sincere heart covenanting was, therefore, crucial to the oath. The English Puritan Cornelius Burges preached in relation to the covenant that "this *joining of ourselves to the Lord*, is such, as is made by *marriage*;...and admits us to the participation of all the most intimate, nearest and choicest expressions of the dearest Love of God, which can be found between the husband and the wife."[92]

Many of Rutherford's letters are written to the nobility of Scotland. He sought to motivate them to use their political influence to further the cause of

---

91. *The Subordinate Standards and Other Authoritative Documents of the Free Church of Scotland* (Edinburgh, 1973), 224–26.

92. Cornelius Burges, *The First Sermon Preached to the House of Commons* (London, 1641), 25.

reformation. In 1648 he published *The Last and Heavenly Speeches, And Glorious Departure of John, Viscount Kenmure* in order to encourage those in Parliament to advance the cause of true religion. In dedicating the pamphlet, Rutherford writes, "For the Whole Nobility of Scotland, and Others Having Voice in Parliament or Committees: God has set you [noblemen] as stars in the firmament of honor;—upon your influence depends the whole course of the inferior world."[93] The narrative is full of the spiritual expressions of felt absence and presence that we associate with Rutherford's letters as well as *Christ Dying, and Drawing Sinners to Himself,* revealing the extent of the influence of this language and experience. The following words were recorded among the last utterances of Kenmure: "Another word was ordinary to him, 'O Son of God, one love-blink, one smack, one kiss of thy mouth, one smile!'" and, "'I will wait on; he is worthy the on-waiting. Though he is long in coming, yet I dare say he is coming, leaping over the mountains, and skipping over the hills: if he were once come we should not sunder.'"[94] Writing from exile in Aberdeen in 1637, Rutherford counsels Lord Loudon, "It were the glory and honor of you who are the nobles of this land, to plead for your wronged Bridegroom and His oppressed spouse, as far as zeal and standing law will go with you."[95] Later he wrote to the Earl of Cassillis,

---

93. In *Anthology of Presbyterian and Reformed Literature*, C. Coldwell, ed. (Dallas: Naphtali Press, 1992), 5:65.

94. Ibid., 77.

95. *Letters*, no. 116, 235. To Alexander Gordon of Earlston he writes, "Ye are the first man in Galloway called out and questioned for

"Oh, if the nobles had done their part, and been zealous for the Lord! It had not been as it is now."[96]

The Confidence of Christian Experience

Adoption has its harvest. It brings forth certain distinguishing fruits, among them hope and prayer. We hope for the inheritance and pray for it, that we may be led unto it. Hope arises from "the feeling of God's love towards us in Christ" and is an "assured waiting for glory to be revealed even under troubles." Troubles themselves are only to make us white and ripe for the Lord's harvest-hook.[97] Hope brings forth its own harvest in this world: the fruits of patience, joy, and holiness.[98]

Although assurance is strengthened by discovering marks of grace within through the work of the Holy Spirit, Christian experience is not self-confident; its confidence is in Christ alone. Samuel Rutherford laid great stress upon the promises of Christ in redemption: "Faith grips the promises and makes us to go out of ourselves to Christ as being homely [familiar] with Him."[99] The promises far outweigh our own changeable feelings, and in many ways, "it is adultery to seek a sign because we cannot rest on our husband's word."[100] True assurance is not something easily obtained; it must be labored after. Rutherford's counsel

---

the name of Jesus.... Howbeit body, life, and goods go for Christ your Lord, and though ye should lose the head for Him" (ibid., no. 59, 133).

96. Ibid., no. 128, 253.
97. Ibid., no. 35, 98.
98. *Catechism*, 62–63.
99. Ibid., 29.
100. *Trial and Triumph*, 34.

is "to give your soul no rest till ye have real assurance, and Christ's rights confirmed and sealed to your soul. The common faith, and country-holiness, and week-day zeal, that is among people, will never bring men to heaven. Take pains for your salvation; for in that day, when ye shall see many men's labors and conquests and idol-riches lying in ashes, when the earth and the works thereof shall be burnt with fire, oh how dear a price would your soul give for God's favor in Christ!"[101]

Rutherford believed that Christians should labor after and seek assurance if they were to go on to maturity. This maturity was not something that was in the essence of saving faith so that one could not be a believer without it. It belonged rather to the exercise of faith. Rutherford argued that if mature assurance was of the essence of saving faith and necessary for salvation, then "none should be justified and saved but the strong believer, whereas Christ died for the weak in the faith."[102] "That faith is essentially a persuasion and assurance of the love of God to me in Christ. 'Tis more than I could ever learn to be the nature of faith, a consequent separable I believe it is."[103]

Because Christian experience has its shadowed depths as well as its rapturous heights, Rutherford sympathized fully with those who labored after assurance that they were in a state of grace, particularly seeking the direct witnessing testimony of the Holy Spirit. Rutherford described the witness of the Spirit as "the voice of God's Spirit accompanying

---

101. *Letters*, no. 190, 374.

102. *Covenant of Life*, 155.

103. *Christ Dying*, 85.

the Word, so speaking to the heart and making all the promises of God to be mine as if the new covenant were written and spoken to me by name."[104] Although convinced that many believers could well attain to this, the godly pastor was aware that some with "weak faith" might never know it, having never a "fair sailing, nor fullness of assurance, until they be upon the shore."[105] Nevertheless, Rutherford exhorts one friend: "Make meikle [much] of assurance, for it keepeth your anchor fixed."[106]

Sanctification and Christian Experience

Assurance and self-examination go hand in hand. Some professing Christians, however, fear examining the work of grace in their soul. They fear that they will become too cast down by focusing on themselves and finding out their shortcomings. This is a mistake, however, for the believer grows in holiness and grace by examining himself. Rutherford warns against a false self-examination that must be avoided. This errs seriously by not looking to Christ and His perfect work.[107] If we look to ourselves without also looking to Christ, we will despair. This work of self-examination is particularly important when we prepare ourselves to partake worthily of the Lord's Supper. "We are to take the candle of God's Word and Spirit into the house of our souls, and to search our mind, will, affections etc.

---

104. *Catechism*, 70.

105. *Influences*, 150.

106. *Letters*, no. 286, 563.

107. Ibid., 84.

and because in the sacrament Christ is to come in, we must put all His enemies, our sins, to the door."[108]

In his catechism, Rutherford gives particular emphasis to sanctification and holiness. The explanations of these doctrines are particularly helpful. He asks, "What are the parts of sanctification?" The answer is direct: "In removing of the stony heart and slaying of sin [mortification], and a quickening of us to love righteousness [vivification]." Rutherford then explains how these aspects of sanctification are found in the experience of the believer. Vivification, or a quickening of the soul to love righteousness, is closely related to the finished work of Christ and the believer's union with Him. "Christ rising from the dead has merited to us newness of life, and His Spirit that raised Him the third day, that death might have no dominion over Him, and that He might ascend to heaven, does quicken us to live to God and seek the things that are above at Christ's right hand."[109]

He defines mortification, or putting sin to death, in an especially vivid way: "For the merit of Christ's death God slays sin and makes us out of sorrow against our sin that slew Christ, and out of love to Jesus who died for us, hate and loathe our sin, so that sorrow and love are the nails that crucify the body of sin."[110] "We must both crucify our lusts by repentance, and fill our hearts with God's love, in whom we may find whatever we seek in pleasure, profit, and honor."[111] One

---

108. Ibid., 81.
109. *Catechism*, 56–57.
110. Ibid., 56.
111. Ibid., 99–100.

example that demonstrates how thorough Rutherford was in exposing sin is his treatment of the guilt of sinful dreams. Some people would object that when we experience sinful dreams we cannot be held responsible and guilty for them because we cannot control our reason and will when we are not fully conscious. Rutherford responds in a clear and practical way: "Sinful dreams are counted our sins, because our vain minds in the day time run upon evil thoughts, and we are not careful by prayer and heavenly meditating to season our hearts with gear [material] which will bring holy dreams in their place."[112]

The Difficulties of Christian Experience

Rutherford emphasizes that even the afflictions of Christian experience are to be seen in relation to Christ and traced to His gracious hand in the midst of our lives. The divine cordial of Romans 8:28 was very real to him: "I bless the Lord, that all our troubles come through Christ's fingers, and that He casteth sugar among them, and casteth in some ounce-weights of heaven, and of the Spirit of glory that resteth on suffering believers, into our cup, in which there is no taste of hell."[113] Rutherford knew well the sorrows of affliction after the death of his first wife and after being deposed from his pulpit and exiled far from all godly friends. While he was engaged at the Westminster Assembly in London, two of his children died. He knew deeply by his own experience the wounds that affliction makes upon the

---

112. Ibid., 99.

113. *Letters*, no. 265, 516.

inward spirit when he sought to counsel others. He writes, "Sorrow, loss, sadness, death, are the worst of things that are, except sin. But Christ knoweth well what to make of them, and can put His own in the cross's common, so that we shall be obliged to affliction, and thank God who taught us to make our acquaintance with such a rough companion, who can hale [draw] us to Christ."[114] In another letter he comments, "I would not want the sweet experience of the consolations of God for all the bitterness of affliction."[115] Rutherford had a true spiritual joy in affliction. The New Testament teaches us in several passages that we should be glad in affliction because it has a precious outcome, and, in light of this, Rutherford emphasizes that "faith hath cause to take courage from our very afflictions; the devil is but a whetstone to sharpen the faith and patience of the saints. I know that he but heweth and polisheth stones, all this time, for the New Jerusalem."[116]

Trials in the church and nation are ordered by Christ's hand for His own glory. He is both seeking out and preparing His bride. In the language of Zechariah 13:9, He is claiming "the third part" through the fires of affliction. "Yet the Lord's third part shall come through the fire, as refined gold for the treasure of the Lord, and the outcasts of Scotland shall be gathered together again, and the wilderness shall blossom as the flower, and bud, and grow as the rose of Sharon; and great shall be the glory of

---

114. Ibid., no. 122, 246.

115. Ibid., no. 11, 52.

116. Ibid., no. 114, 231.

the Lord upon Scotland."[117] Rutherford believed in the importance of seeking to understand the dispensations of God in providence and that nothing was without its significance. "The condition of the people of God in the three kingdoms calleth for this, that we now wisely consider what the Lord is doing. There is a language of the Lord's 'fire in Zion,' and 'his furnace in Jerusalem,' if we could understand the voice of the crying rod."[118]

Rutherford knew sore trials both in church and state. When Cromwell defeated the Scots army resoundingly at Dunbar in 1650, Rutherford found it an extreme affliction: "I have suffered much," he wrote, "but this is the thickest darkness...I have yet [known]."[119] During the 1650s Cromwell proceeded to keep Scotland under his control, intervening in the affairs of the church, such as ordinations, and prohibiting general assemblies. Although invited to take up professorships at Edinburgh University and in Holland, Rutherford believed that his place was at St. Andrews, seeking to uphold the cause of Christ in Scotland.

During this time Rutherford also knew the heartbreak of a severe split that tore the Church of Scotland apart and kept him from the fellowship of true Christians. Christ's most beloved ones and foremost servants are often the sorest afflicted and tried: The "lintel-stone and pillars of the New Jerusalem suffer more knocks of God's hammer and tool

---

117. Ibid., no. 176, 333.

118. *Trial and Triumph*, 7.

119. *Letters*, no. 330, 653.

St. Andrews University, where Rutherford was
appointed to the position of professor of theology in 1639;
in 1651, he was appointed rector,
and he spent the last fourteen years of his
life teaching and preaching there.

than the common side-wall stones."[120] Rutherford believed it was necessary to defend the truth and not to give away one hair's-breadth of it, but he lamented the sad effects of controversy and church divisions such as diminished spiritual appetite and fervor. As he observed in a polemic against Thomas Hooker's congregationalism, "When the head is filled with topics and none of the flamings of Christ's love in the heart, how dry are all disputes. For too often, fervor of dispute in the head weakens love in the heart. And what can our paper-industry add to the spotless truth of our Lord Jesus?"[121]

The Future of Christian Experience

Christian experience has a past, present, and future. When we remember "mercies, deliverances, rods, warnings…consolations…manifestations of God… experiences, answers from the Lord," we may be "comforted now" concerning the Lord's goodwill toward us, but also "confirmed in the certain hope, that grace, free grace, in a fixed and established Surety, shall perfect that good work in you."[122] All that we experience now makes us long all the more for the time when it will be possible to enjoy our God and Redeemer without sinning for all eternity. Rutherford expresses a yearning for that day: "O for eternity's leisure to look on Him, to feast upon a sight of His face. O for the long summer-day of endless

---

120. Ibid., no. 112, 228.

121. Samuel Rutherford, *A Survey of the Survey of that Summe of Church Discipline penned by Mr Thomas Hooker* (London: Printed by J. G. for Andr. Crook, 1658), sig. A2.

122. *Letters*, no. 341, 674.

ages to stand beside Him and enjoy Him! O time,
O sin, be removed out of the way. O day, O fairest
of days, dawn! O morning of eternity, break out,
and arise, that we may enjoy this incomprehensible
Lord."[123] Rutherford realizes that at present, in the
limitations of our sinful state, we cannot know the
fullness of Christian experience and all that will be
our portion in glory: "Would Christ in His fullness
of the irradiations of His glory break in upon us, He
should break the bodily organs, and over-master the
soul's faculties, that all the banks of the soul should be
like broken walls, hedges or clay channels;... we must
be both more capacious, and wider and stronger vessels, before we be made fit to contain glory."[124] Soon
Rutherford was to enter into the fullness of what he
had experienced in foretaste upon this earth.

When Charles II was restored to the throne of
Great Britain in 1660, various prominent Covenanters were identified for punishment. The Committee
of Estates in Scotland issued a declaration against
Rutherford's book *Lex, Rex*, which had been written
in opposition to absolute monarchy, and copies of
the book were burned in Edinburgh and outside New
College in St. Andrews. Rutherford was deprived of
his position in the university, his charge in the church,
and his stipend, and he was confined to his own
house. He was cited to appear before Parliament on a
charge of treason, and his friends feared that he might
well face execution in common with some of the other
more prominent Covenanters. Early in 1661 Ruther-

---

123. *Sermon Preached...Commons* (Edinburgh, 1644), 46.
124. *Christ Dying*, 45.

ford fell seriously ill, however. When the summons came in 1661, charging him with treason and demanding his appearance on a certain day, Rutherford answered from his deathbed, "I have got summons already before a superior Judge and Judicatory, and I behove to answer to my first summons, and ere your day come, I will be where few kings and great folks come."[125] His exhortations to the company of ministers that gathered around his deathbed could be taken as a summary of his own life. "My Lord and Master is chief of ten thousands of thousands. None is comparable to Him, in heaven or in earth. Dear brethren, do all for Him. Pray for Christ. Preach for Christ. Do all for Christ; beware of men-pleasing." Before he died he said, "This night will close the door and fasten my anchor within the veil." His last recorded words were, "Glory, glory dwelleth in Immanuel's Land."[126] Rutherford writes longingly of eternal life with his Lord:

Oh, how sweet to be wholly Christ's, and wholly in Christ! To be out of the creature's owning and made complete in Christ! to live by faith in Christ and to be, once for all, clothed with the uncreated majesty and glory of the Son of God, wherein He maketh all His friends and followers sharers! To dwell in Immanuel's high and blessed land, and live in that sweetest air where no wind bloweth but the breathings of the Holy Ghost, no seas or floods flow but the pure water of life that proceedeth from under the throne and from the Lamb! No planting but the Tree of Life that yieldeth twelve manner of

---

125. Rutherford, *Letters* (1905), 38.
126. *Letters*, 21–22.

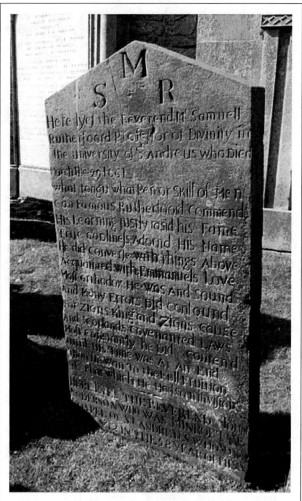

Rutherford's grave at the Old
Cathedral graveyard in St. Andrews.

Photo courtesy of Douglas Bond.

fruits every month! What do we here but sin and
suffer? Oh, when shall the night be gone, the shadows flee away and the morning of that long, long
day without cloud or night, dawn?[127]

This was his greatest desire: "I would seek no
more to make me happy for evermore, but a thorough
and clear sight of the beauty of Jesus my Lord. Let my
eyes enjoy His fairness, and stare Him forever in the
face, and I have all that can be wished."[128] At the foot
of the ruined wall of the cathedral of St. Andrews,
Rutherford's gravestone describes his passion for
Christ and the fulfillment of his greatest desire:

> True godliness adorned his name,
> He did converse with things above,
> Acquainted with Emmanuel's love....
> Mostly constantly he did contend
> Until his time was at an end.
> Then he won to the full fruition
> Of that which he had seen in vision.[129]

---

127. Ibid., no. 333, 661–62.

128. Ibid., no. 202, 398.

129. T. Campbell, *Standing Witnesses: A Guide to the Scottish Covenanters and Their Memorials with a Historical Introduction* (Edinburgh:
Saltire Society, 1996), 169. The full text of the epitaph is recorded here.

The manse where Rutherford lived when
he was minister at Anwoth.

1

Believing the Scriptures[1]

*For as yet they knew not the scripture, that he must
rise again from the dead.*
— John 20:9

The rest of the disciples did not believe these Scriptures that foretold of Christ's resurrection from the dead. Can it be possible that there can be a scholar in Christ's school who has not learned his lesson that Christ taught him? Can it be that any who have heard Christ Himself make so many preachings of His resurrection would not believe, for all that? Aye, you may see the proof of it here.

The doctrine that arises from this is clear: that it is neither the means nor hearing Christ as a man preach out of His own mouth that will do the turn[2] and bring us to God and make us understand spiritual things. Preaching, indeed, is God's means that He has appointed for that end and the way that He ordains for bringing in souls to Him. But when all is done, it is not the only means of bringing us to Him. The special thing is that which is spoken by our Savior Himself, that wind that "bloweth where it listeth," and no man knows "whence it cometh, and whither it goeth"

---

1. *Quaint Sermons*, 71–73.

2. *do the turn:* perform the work

(John 3:8). We may preach to you until our head breaks and our breasts burst; aye, we may preach to you until doomsday, and yet that will not do the turn unless the inward calling of the Spirit is joined with it. For an outward sound to the ear is one thing, and Christ's loosing all knots and removing all impediments another thing. Christ Himself said while He was in the flesh, "No man can come to me, except the Father…draw him" (John 6:44). Christ is speaking in that place to those who had the outward means, and yet, He says, it is not a strange thing that they do not come to Him, even though they have the means, because they lack the Father's draught[3] to draw them to Him. The scribes often heard Christ preach, and yet for all that, they consented to the slaying of the Lord of glory (1 Cor. 2:8).

Christ is preached there both to the Jew and to the Gentile, and yet, for all that, to the Jew He is a stumbling block, and to the Greek, the preaching of Christ is foolishness. We have much to do when the Lord's Word is preached to pray to Him that He would join His Spirit and His wind with His Word. Aye, all of our own means or those of others are nothing without that being joined. It is in vain for us to rise early and lie down late and eat the bread of sorrow all day, if the Lord does not give the assistance of His Spirit to the means that we use.

And again, we may learn from this that arms of men are not the thing that will save us if the Lord Himself does not watch over the camp. God keeps evermore the issue and the event of all things in His

---

3. *draught:* pulling motion or action

own hand. And this serves to teach us not to trust in means of any sort, whether it be inward or outward matters. We should not trust in man or in weapons or any second causes whatsoever, but only in the Lord Himself, who is the only strength of His people. And so learn to overlook second causes when you look that way, and look no lower than heaven, to Him who sits there and guides and overrules all battles in the world and all things else, and will let it be seen in the end salvation—salvation, even His salvation to all those who trust in Him.

2

The Messenger of the Covenant[1]

The LORD, whom ye seek, shall suddenly come to his temple, even the messenger of the covenant, whom ye delight in.

—Malachi 3:1

Christ travels with tidings between the parties.[2]

1. He reports of God to us—that it is His Father's will that we be saved (John 6:39).

2. Christ reports of Himself, for it sets[3] Christ to be a broker[4] for Himself and for Wisdom to cry in the streets, "Who will have me?" (Prov. 1:20–22; 9:1–5). It became[5] the Lord Jesus to praise Himself: "I am that bread of life"; "I am the light of the world"; "I am the door"; and "I am the good shepherd" (John 6:48; 8:12; 10:9, 11).

3. He praises His Father: "My Father is the husbandman" (John 15:1).

---

1. *Trial and Triumph*, sermon 7, 77–78.

2. Earlier in the sermon, Rutherford explained that the two parties are God, and Christ the Mediator along with His children.

3. *sets:* is fitting for

4. *broker:* the middleman in a business transaction

5. *became:* was fitting for

4. He suits us in marriage and commends His Father, our Father-in-Law. "You marry me, dear souls. Oh, but my Father is a great person. In my Father's house are many mansions" (John 14:2).

He commends us to the Father; a messenger making peace will do this. "They have received [thy words], and have known surely that I came out from thee, and they have believed that thou didst send me" (John 17:8). "O righteous Father, the world hath not known thee: but I have known thee, and these have known that thou hast sent me" (John 17:25). Ministers cannot speak of Christ and His Father as He can Himself. Oh, come! Hear Christ, speak of Christ, and of His Father, and of heaven, for He saw all. O sweet believer! Christ gives you a good report in heaven; the Father and the Son are speaking of you behind backs. A good report in heaven is of much esteem; Christ spoke more good of you than you are worth. He tells over again Ephraim's prayers behind his back (Jer. 31:18). Oh, woe to you when Christ is telling black tidings of you in heaven! Such a man will not believe in Me; he hates Me and My cause and My people. Christ cannot lie about any man.

The wooded path between the manse and the church
at Anwoth, still called Rutherford's Walk.

3

Lost Sheep[1]

*I am not sent but unto the lost
sheep of the house of Israel.*
—Matthew 15:24

First, a word of sheep, then of "lost sheep." I give
no other reasons why the redeemed of the Lord are
called sheep than are obvious in Scripture. Sheep are
passive creatures and can do little for themselves, just
as believers in the work of their salvation, such as:

1. Of themselves, believers do not have more knowledge of the saving way than sheep, and so they cannot
walk but as they are taught and led. "Teach me, O
LORD" (Ps. 119:33). "Lead me in thy truth" (Ps.
25:5). (1) Like a blind man holding out his hand to
his guide, so are believers: "Lead me, O LORD, in thy
righteousness" (Ps. 5:8). (2) This is not common leading, but the leading used with children, as someone
teaches them to walk by holding onto them. "When
Ephraim [Israel] was a child, then I loved him" (Hos.
11:1). "I taught Ephraim also to go, taking them by
their arms"; but Ephraim, like a child, did not know
his leader: "But they knew not," says the Lord, "that
I healed them" (Hos. 11:3). (3) Leading may suppose some willingness, but we must be drawn: "No

<hr>

1. *Trial and Triumph*, sermon 13, 134–35.

man can come to me, except the Father...draw him" (John 6:44). "Draw me, we will run after thee" (Song 1:4). (4) There is a word of special grace, which is more than teaching, leading, and drawing, and that is "leaning": "Who is this that cometh up from the wilderness, leaning upon her beloved?" (Song 8:5). (5) There is a word yet more, and that is "bearing": when the Good Shepherd has found the lost sheep, "he layeth it on his shoulders, rejoicing" (Luke 15:5). "Hearken unto me, O house of Jacob, and all the remnant of the house of Israel, which are borne by me from the belly, which are carried from the womb" (Isa. 46:3). So also, "[God] beareth them on [eagles'] wings" (Deut. 32:11). Grace, grace is a noble guide and tutor.

2. The life of sheep is the most dependent life in the world; there are no such dependent creatures as sheep. All their happiness is the goodness, care, and wisdom of their shepherd. Wolves, lions, and leopards need none to watch over them. Briars and thorns grow alone; the vine tree, the noble vine, is a tender thing, and must be supported. Christ must bear the weak and lambs in His bosom (Isa. 40:11). The Shepherd's bosom and His legs are the legs of the weak lamb. Even the habit of grace[2] is created and is no independent thing, and so, in its creation, in its preservation, it depends on Christ. Grace is as the newborn bird; its life is the heat and warmness of

---

2. "Habit" comes from the Latin *habitus*, meaning "state." Scholastic theology distinguished between God's grace as acts or influences upon the believer and as a created habit within the soul, that is, a new nature or state of grace.

the body and wings of the dam.[3] It is like a chariot; though it has four wheels, yet it moves only as it is drawn by the strength of horses without it. It is a plough made of timber only, without iron and steel, that does not break up the earth. The new seed of God acts as it is acted upon by God; hence, repenting Ephraim says, "Turn thou me, and I shall be turned" (Jer. 31:18). Renewed David is often at this: "Quicken me, quicken me." The swooning church says, "Stay me with flagons, comfort me with apples" (Song 2:5).

3. Sheep are docile creatures. "My sheep hear my voice, and I know them, and they follow me" (John 10:27). There is a controversy with Papists over how we know that Scripture is the Word of God. There are two things here worthy of consideration—one within, and another without. How does the lamb know its mother among a thousand of the flock? Natural instinct teaches it. From what teacher or art is it that the swallow builds its clay house and nest, and every bee knows its own cell and waxen house? So the instinct of grace knows the voice of the Beloved among many voices (Song 2:8). And this discerning power is in the subject. There is another power in the object. Of many thousand millions of men since the creation, not one, in figure and shape, is altogether like another; there is some visible difference. Among many voices, there is no voice like man's tongue. Among millions of diverse tongues of men, every voice has an audible difference printed on it, by which it is discerned from all others. To the new creature, there is in Christ's Word some character, some sound

---

3. *dam:* mother

of heaven that is in no voice in the world, but in His only. In Christ, as He is represented to a believer's eye of faith, there is a shape and a stamp of divine majesty; no man knows it but the believer, and in heaven and earth Christ has not a marrow[4] like Himself. Suppose there were a hundred counterfeit moons or fancied suns in the heaven; a natural eye can discern the true moon and the natural sun from them all. The eye knows white is not black or green. Christ, offered to the eye of faith, stamps little images of Himself, that the soul dare go to death and to hell with it, that this, this only was Christ, and none other but He only.

4. Sheep are simple: they are often led by their fancy,[5] and therefore they are straying creatures (Isa. 53:6; Ps. 119:176; 1 Peter 2:25). There is nothing of the notion of death or of another life in the fancy of sheep; a mouthful of green grass carries the sheep into a pit and into the mouth and teeth of lions and wolves. Fancy is often the guide of weak believers rather than faith; by nature, we care little for what we shall be in the next generation. Fancy and nature cannot out-see time or see over or beyond death. Fair green-like hopes of gain are to us hopes of real good: we think we see two moons in one heaven. There is a way that seems good that deceives us, but black death is the night lodging of it. Alas! We are journeying, and we do not know where our inns for the night are and where we shall lodge when the sun is going down. Poor soul! Where shall you be all night?

---

4. *marrow:* match, or another identical or equal person of the same kind

5. *fancy:* imaginations

4

Sorrow for Sin[1]

I have surely heard Ephraim bemoaning himself.
—Jeremiah 31:18

Ephraim, God's dear child, is brought in, as com-
mended of God, and the Lord tells over and over
again about Ephraim's prayers and sorrowing for sin:
"I have surely heard Ephraim bemoaning himself"
(Jer. 31:18).

1. We have a precept for it in the New Testament:
"Be afflicted, and mourn, and weep: let your laughter
be turned to mourning, and your joy to heaviness.
Humble yourselves in the sight of the Lord, and he
shall lift you up" (James 4:9–10). Now, they had
better reason to mourn for sin because they did lust,
war, and were contentious than because there were
afflictions on them. Nature will cause any to cry
when punishment is on them; not nature but grace,
not the flesh but the Spirit causes men sorrow for
sin as sin: "If then their uncircumcised hearts be
humbled, and they then accept of the punishment
of their iniquity: then will I remember my covenant
with Jacob" (Lev. 26:41–42).

---

1. *Trial and Triumph*, sermon 17, 190–92, 94.

2. To mourn for sin is a grace promised under the New Testament: "And I will pour upon the house of David, and upon the inhabitants of Jerusalem, the spirit of grace and of supplications, and they shall look upon me whom they have pierced, and they shall mourn for him, as one mourneth for his only son" (Zech. 12:10).

3. Those for whom the consolations of Christ are ordained are the mourners in Zion; but the consolations of Christ are not for legal mourners and such as are weary and laden for sin and yet never come to Christ or believe. There is no promise made to such mourners as Cain and Judas were. Can we say that God promises grace and mercy to any acts of the flesh or of unbelief?

4. It is a mark of a conscience in a right frame[2] to be affected with a sense of the least[3] sin, as David was one in whose conscience there remained the character of a stripe[4] when he but cut the lap of Saul's robe (1 Sam. 24).

5. And when wicked men sin, their conscience is past feeling (Eph. 4:19) and seared as with a hot iron (1 Tim. 4:2). It is not an argument of faith, understanding the meaning of sin pardoned, not to mourn for sin and confess it.... Justified Job says, "If I wash myself with snow water, and make my hands never so clean; yet shalt thou plunge me in the ditch, and mine own clothes shall abhor me" (Job 9:30–31).

---

2. *frame:* condition

3. *least:* smallest

4. *stripe:* the mark left by a lash

"Behold, I am vile; what shall I answer thee?" (Job 40:4). This is what Job says, after he was by God's pen declared an upright man, of his own ways in his sufferings. And David, a justified man, says, "Enter not into judgment with thy servant: for in thy sight shall no man living be justified" (Ps. 143:2). Yet Job and David were no hypocrites.

5

Unsearchable Grace[1]

O the depth of the riches both of the wisdom and knowledge of God! how unsearchable are his judgments, and his ways past finding out!
                                              —Romans 11:33

Paul shows that God has committed all to unbelief, that He might have mercy on all (Rom. 11:32). He shows a reason why the Lord was pleased to cast off His ancient people for a time and to ingraft the Gentiles, the wild olive, in their place in saying, "O the depth!" (Rom. 11:32). He cannot find any reason other than the bottomless and unsearchable freedom of grace and free dispensation to some people and persons, and not to others. I confess it would not be such depth if the Lord from eternity had equally loved all to salvation, but, because of the creature's running and willing or his not-running and not-willing, had later been urged by wiser and riper thoughts and a consequent will to save or not save, as men and angels in the high and indifferent court of their free will shall think good. In this case there would be no other depth than is in earthly judges, who reward well-doers and punish ill-doers, or in a

---

1. *Christ Dying*, 543–45.

lord of a vineyard who gives wages to him that labors and no wages to him that stands idle and does nothing.

This would be the law of nature, of nations, and no depth; it would be God rewarding men according to their works and showing mercy to those who cooperate with and improve well the benefit of God's antecedent will and not showing mercy to those who do not cooperate with His will, but out of the absoluteness of indifferent freewill fail to make use of the benefit of God's will.[2] But the great and unsearchable depth is the way in which God should so carry on the great designs of the declaration of the glory of pardoning mercy and punishing justice, as there should be some persons and nations who are chosen and must obey the gospel and be called, without any respect to works, but of grace (Rom. 11:5–7; Rom. 9:11), as He did with the Jews first, and not the Gentiles, as of old; and now the Gentiles are taken into Christ and the Jews are cast off; and again,…both Jews and Gentiles…. Now, in both these,

1. God is free in His grace.

2. He is just in His judgments, though He neither calls nor chooses according to works.

3. The damned creature is most guilty.

4. The Lord is both justly severe and graciously merciful.

5. None have cause to complain or quarrel with God, and yet God might have carried out the matter an entirely different way.

---

2. Rutherford uses irony in referring to Arminian terms here.

6. The head cause of this various administration, with nations and persons, is the deep, high, sovereign, innocent, holy, independent will of the Great Potter and Former of all things, who has mercy on whom He will and hardens whom He will; and this is the depth without a bottom.

No creatures—angels or men—can behave in this way to their fellow creatures and still be free, just, holy, wise, etc., but one creature can deal with his fellow creature according to the rules and roadway of an antecedent and consequent will, as a king may deal with his people, a governor with those he governs, a father with his children, a commander with his soldiers, a lord of a vineyard with his hired servants. All these may order their goodness, mercy, rewards, and punishments in a way that is befitting the use, industry, and improvement of free will or the rebellion, injustice, wickedness, and slothfulness of their underlings. But no master or lord can call laborers to his vineyard and exhort, obtest,[3] beseech them all to labor, and promise them hire and yet keep from the greatest part of them the power of freely stirring their arms or legs to labor and suspend his acting on them so that they shall willingly be carried on to willful disobedience and be the passive objects of his revenging justice, according to the lord's determinate counsel, because he willed out of his absolute sovereignty to deal this way with some and deal a just contrary way with the least part of the laborers because he purposed to declare the glory of his grace on them. Either there is an unsearchable depth here, or Paul knew nothing.

---

3. *obtest:* testify to or supplicate

Archibald Campbell, Marquis of Argyll (1607–1661),
intervened on Rutherford's behalf when he was
tried in an ecclesiastical court for writing against
the Arminian errors of Archbishop Laud.

6

The Soul Trouble of the Redeemer[1]

Now is my soul troubled; and what shall I say?
Father, save me from this hour: but for this cause
came I unto this hour. Father, glorify thy name.
— John 12:27–28

In the complaint, we have the Lord's troubled soul.
This holy soul thus troubled was like the earth before
the Fall—before it was cursed—out of which grew
roses without thorns or thistles. Christ's anger and His
sorrow were flowers that smelled of heaven, and not of
sin. All His affections[2] of fear, sorrow, sadness, hope,
joy, love, and desire were like a fountain of liquid and
melted silver, of which the banks, the head spring, are
all as clear from dross as pure crystal. Such a fountain
can cast out no clay, no mud, no dirt. When His affections did rise and swell into His actions, every drop of
the fountain was sinless, perfumed and adorned with
grace, just as the more you stir or trouble a well of rose
water or some precious liquor, the more sweet a smell
it casts out, or when a summer soft wind blows on a
field of sweet roses, it diffuses precious and delicious
smells through the air.

---

1. *Christ Dying*, 3–4.

2. *affections:* emotions

There are mud and dregs in the bottom and banks of our affections, so that when our anger, sorrow, sadness, and fear do arise in their actions, our fountain casts out sin. We cannot love without lust; or fear, but we despair; nor rejoice, but we are wanton and vain and gaudy; nor believe, but we presume. We reft[3] up, we breathe out sin, we cast out a smell of hell when the wind blows on our field of weeds and thistles. Our soul is just a plot of wild corn, the imaginations of our heart being only evil from our youth. Oh that Christ would plant some of His flowers in our soul and bless the soil that they might grow kindly there, being warmed and nourished with His grace! If grace is within, it comes out under the pressures of sadness. A saint is a saint in affliction, as a hypocrite is a hypocrite; every man is himself and casts a smell like himself when he is in the furnace. Troubled Christ prays. Tempted Job believes (Job 19:25). The scourged apostles rejoice (Acts 5:41). Drowned Jonah looks to the holy temple (Jonah 2:4).

Christ's affections were rational; reason started up before fear. Reason and affection did not outrun one another. Grace did so accompany nature that He could not have any more fear than the object required. Neither were His affections above banks. He saw the blackest and darkest hour that ever any saw. If all the sufferings of the damned, for eternity, were before them in one sight or came on them at once, it would annihilate all who are now, or shall be, in hell. Christ now saw, or foresaw, as great sufferings as these, and

---

3. *reft:* A variant spelling of *rift*, meaning "to emit from the mouth, as by belching."

yet (1) believed, (2) prayed, (3) hoped, (4) was encouraged under it, (5) suffered them to the bottom with all patience, (6) rejoiced in hope (Ps. 16:9).

Our affections rise and swell before reason. (1) They are often imaginary and are on horseback and in arms at the stirring of a straw. (2) They lack that clearness and serenity of grace that Christ had, through habitual grace following nature from the womb. (3) We can raise our affections but cannot allay them, as some can make war and cannot create peace.

Christ had now and always the grace of peace, as peace is opposed to culpable raging of conscience. First, He never could lack faith, which is a serenity, quietness, and silence of the soul and assurance of the love of God. Second, He could have no doubting or sinful disturbance of mind because He could have no conscience of guilt that could cloud over the love and most tender favor of His Father to Him. Christ never needed pardon; He never needed the grace of forgiveness, or grace to be spared. God did not spare Him. God could exact no less blood of Him than He shed, but He received an acquittal of justification, never a pardon of grace. He lacked the peace that is opposed to pain and the sense of wrath and punishment for the guilt of our sins, but He was now under penal disturbance and disquietness of soul.

7

The Mystery of
Christ's Soul Trouble[1]

*Now is my soul troubled; and what shall I say?
Father, save me from this hour: but for this cause
came I unto this hour. Father, glorify thy name.*
—John 12:27–28

The cause of this soul trouble was for sinners; this was
surety[2] suffering. The choicest and most stately piece
that God ever created and dearest to God, second
only to God-man, was the princely soul of Christ. It
was a king's soul. Yet death, by reason of sin, came
upon it. It was not a common death, but that which is
the marrow[3] of death, the firstborn and the strongest
of deaths, enduring the wrath of God and the innocent pain of hell, yet void of despair and hatred of
God. If I had any hell to endure, I should choose an
innocent hell like Christ's. Better suffer ill a thousand
times than sin; suffering is rather to be chosen than
sin. It was pain, and nothing but pain. Damned men
and reprobate devils are not capable of a godly and

1. *Christ Dying*, 11–13.

2. *surety:* one who has become legally liable for the debt, default,
or failure in duty of another

3. *marrow:* essence

innocent hell; they cannot choose to suffer hell and not spit on fair and spotless justice. Because Christ's blood was to wash away sin, He could not both fully pay and contract debt also.

But if it is so that death, finding so precious a surety as Christ's princely and sinless soul, made Him obey the law of the land before He escaped from the land, what wonder is it that we who are born in the land of death die? There is no creature that does not travail in pain, with death in its bosom or an inclination to mother-nothing,[4] from where it came. Only God stands between the mightiest angel in heaven and nothing. All things under the moon must have been sick from vanity and death if the Heir of all things, coming in among dying creatures, out of dispensation, by law had to die. If the Lord's soul, and the soul of such a Lord, had to die and suffer wrath, then let the fair face of the world, the heavens, look like the face of an old man, full of trembling, white hairs, and wrinkles (Ps. 102:26). Then let man make for his long home; let time itself wax old and gray-haired. Why should I desire to stay here when Christ had to pass away?

And if this spotless soul that never sinned was troubled, what wonder, then, that there are many troubles for the sinner? Our Savior, who promises soul rest to others, cannot have soul rest Himself. His soul is now sorely tossed on a wheel, and all creatures are on a wheel and in motion. There is not a creature since Adam sinned that sleeps soundly. Weariness

---

4. *mother-nothing:* A phrase coined by Rutherford referring to the fact that all things have been created out of nothing.

and motion is laid on the moon and sun and all creatures on this side of the moon. Seas ebb and flow, and
that's trouble; winds blow, and rivers move. For five
thousand years, heavens and stars, except one time,
have not had six minutes' rest.[5] Living creatures walk
toward death. Kingdoms and cities are on the wheel
of changes, up and down. Mankind runs and is troubled by diseases of the body and soul trouble.... Men
are motion sick.... The six-day creation has been
travailing and shouting in pain, and the child has not
been born yet (Rom. 8:22). This poor woman [the
whole creation] has been groaning under the bondage
of vanity and shall not be brought to bed to give birth
until Jesus comes the second time to be midwife. All
the great of heaven and earth, since God laid the first
stone of this wide hall, have been groaning and weeping for the liberty of the sons of God (Rom. 8:21). The
figure of the passing-away world is like an old man's
face, full of wrinkles and foul with weeping (1 Cor.
7:31). We are waiting for the time when Jesus will be
revealed from heaven and will come and wipe the old
man's face. All creatures here are on their feet; none
of them can sit or lie.

Christ's soul now is above trouble and rests sweetly
in the bosom of God. Troubled souls, rejoice in hope.
Soft and childish saints do not take it well when they
are not feasted every day with Christ's love.... But
since the fairest piece of the man Jesus, His precious
soul, was sick with soul trouble, and since the noble
and renowned Head Heir of all, the first of His kingly
house, uttered deep groans that pierced skies and

_____
5. See Joshua 10:12.

heaven and rent the rocks, why should sinners fail to
be submissive when Christ is pleased to set children
down to walk on foot and hide Himself from them?
But they forget the difference between the inns of clay
and the home of glory. Our fields here are sown with
tears; grief grows in every furrow of this lowland.
You shall lay soul and head down in the bosom...of
Jesus Christ; that bed must be soft and delicious. It
is perfumed with uncreated glory. When Christ shall
circle His glorious arm about your head and you rest
in an infinite compass of surpassing glory; when glory
or ripened grace shall be with you and without you,
above and below; when your feet of clay shall walk
upon pure surpassing glory, the thoughts of all your
soul troubles now shall be as shadows that passed
away ten thousand years ago.

8

The Beloved Withdraws[1]

I rose up to open to my beloved...but my beloved had withdrawn himself, and was gone.
— Song of Solomon 5:5–6

There are two things here for us to consider that prove how wounding sins are against the love of Christ.

1. "My beloved hath withdrawn himself." The text is, "And my beloved had turned about." Because Christ is unwilling to remove Himself and wholly go away, He only turned aside. This intimates that Christ does not take a direct journey to go away and leave His own children. He goes aside from the door of the soul only a little to testify He would gladly, with His soul, come in. What ingratitude is it to shut Him away violently?

2. "My soul failed." The old version is, "My soul melted at His speaking." My soul passed over, or went away. To remember His ravishing words broke my life and made me die: that is, I remembered a world of love in Him when He knocked, saying, "Open to me, my sister, my love, my dove." To sin against so great a bond as grace must be the sin of

---

1. *Christ Dying*, 18–19.

sins and among the highest sins, as is clear in those that sin against the Holy Ghost. Then it must be impossible to give grace anything. We can only pay our debts to grace; we cannot give the debt of grace to grace in the whole sum.

The Market Cross at Aberdeen. Rutherford was banished
to Aberdeen for twenty-two months for writing a book
against Archbishop Laud's Arminianism.

9

Confession of Sin[1]

If we confess our sins, he is faithful and just to forgive us our sins, and to cleanse us from all unrighteousness.
—1 John 1:9

For confession, there are (1) commandment, (2) practice, and (3) promise.

1. "Speak unto the children of Israel, when a man or woman shall commit any sin that men commit, to do a trespass against the LORD, and that person be guilty; then they shall confess their sin which they have done" (Num. 5:6–7). This is not a duty of the unconverted only, but an obligation for all the children of Israel, men and women. "Confess your faults one to another" (James 5:16). Now, our confession is not made to men only, as if the sins that the justified person commits were only before men and not in the court of heaven before God, as libertines teach; therefore, it is added, "Confess...and pray one for another, that ye may be healed. The effectual fervent prayer of a righteous man availeth much." Therefore, justified persons are to pray for pardon of confessed sins. I take it to be a precept that as many as say "Our Father" to God in prayer should also say, "Forgive

---

1. *Trial and Triumph*, sermon 17, 188–89.

us our sins, as we forgive them that sin against us."
And so we justified people who are sons of God
should ask for pardon of sins when we pray for daily
bread and the coming of Christ's kingdom: "Take
with you words, and turn to the LORD: say unto him,
Take away all iniquity" (Hos. 14:2). This must be a
confession—that a people turned to the Lord are in
their iniquities.

2. This is set down as a commendable practice: Ezra
confessed and wept (Ezra 10:1). "And the seed of
Israel separated themselves from all strangers, and
stood and confessed their sins, and the iniquities of
their fathers" (Neh. 9:2). "I prayed unto the LORD
my God, and made my confession" (Dan. 9:4).
And David says, "I have sinned against the LORD"
(2 Sam. 12:13). The church confesses, "Thou art
wroth; for we have sinned.... But we are all as an
unclean thing" (Isa. 64:5–6). "For our transgressions
are multiplied before thee, and our sins testify against
us" (Isa. 59:12). "I have sinned..., O thou preserver
of man" (Job 7:20). "Mine iniquities...are more [in
number] than the hairs of mine head" (Ps. 40:12).
"Our iniquities testify against us..., our backslidings
are many" (Jer. 14:7).

It is a vain shift[2] to say, "The church prays and
confesses for the wicked party, not for the justified
ones." For as many as were afflicted confessed their
sins, for which the hand of God was upon them. Now
God's hand was upon all: Daniel and Jeremiah were
carried away captive—indeed, the whole seed of
Jacob (Isa. 42:24–25; 64:5–7). And Jeremiah, in the

---

2. *shift:* evasion

name of the whole captive church, says, "The LORD is righteous; for I have rebelled against his commandment" (Lam. 1:18).

There is a promise made to these that confess: "Whoso confesseth and forsaketh [his sins] shall have mercy" (Prov. 28:13). "When I kept silence [and did not confess] my bones waxed old.... I said, I will confess my transgression unto the LORD; and thou forgavest the iniquity of my sin" (Ps. 32:3, 5). And this is not an Old Testament spirit only; for this is the same promise: "If we confess our sins, he is faithful and just to forgive" (1 John 1:9). "If they shall confess their iniquity,...then will I remember my covenant with Jacob" (Lev. 26:40, 42). Not to confess is shown to be guiltiness: "Yet thou sayest, Because I am innocent, surely his anger shall turn from me. Behold, I will plead with thee, because thou sayest, I have not sinned" (Jer. 2:35). It is a token of impenitency: "No man repented him of his wickedness, saying, What have I done?" (Jer. 8:6).

10

The Hand of the Beloved at the Door of the Heart[1]

My beloved put in his hand by the hole of the door.
—Song of Solomon 5:4

"My beloved put in his hand"—that is, with the outward ministry of the Word. He put in His hand—which is His Spirit (Acts 11:21; Ezek. 3:14; Luke 11:20)—in the hole of my heart, to make a wider hole. I confess this putting of Christ's hand in the keyhole of the heart is better felt than told. But it is this: when Christ sent His voice and tongue through the door, it did not [do] the work, and therefore He caused His hand to follow His tongue. He gave with the hand of His Spirit such a blow, until bed and house and all did shake, and the door fell on the floor. Does anyone who knows Christ's working not know this—that when Christ speaks, His Spirit will make in the heart a stirring and such a glowing, that they will find His soft hand rubbing their cold heart? And when a key and lock are rusted, we rub oil upon the rusty part. When Christ comes, He finds the wards,[2]

---

1. *Quaint Sermons*, 91–93.

2. *ward:* projecting ridge of metal in a lock casing or keyhole permitting only the insertion of a key with a corresponding notch

sprents[3] go in and out at will, and He takes will and heart and affections in His hand and scours them with His file. "I am apprehended of Christ Jesus" (Phil. 3:12). "Did not our heart burn within us, while he talked with us?" (Luke 24:32). "He brought me to the banqueting house" (Song 2:4). This was a pull of Christ, taking her by the shoulders and bringing her into the king's pantry.

Hence, here are two actions. One of the Word— painting out with alluring and soul-delighting words Christ's fair white and ruddy face; this is a moral yoke. And withal there is a real action of the hand of the Spirit in all His ten fingers working upon the lock and setting, engraving, and stamping Christ in deep letters upon the soul. As when a fish is taken there are two actions, the bait alluring and beguiling the fish with hope of meat. This is like the working of the Word, which is Christ's bait; but when He wins us to dry land, then, when the fish is hooked, there is a real action of the fisher, drawing and hauling the fish to land; it leaps and flutters and wrestles while it bleeds with the hook. And this answers to the Holy Spirit's powerful hauling and drawing of the soul in all the affections, that the soul feels joy, comfort, delight, desire, longing, and believing, while nibbling and biting Christ's bait.

---

3. *sprent:* work of the lock

11

Spiritual Lethargy[1]

*I have put off my coat; how shall I put it on? I have
washed my feet; how shall I defile them?*
—Song of Solomon 5:3

There is a dispute here with chiding. "Is not this,"
would she say, "an unreasonable suit of my well
beloved to bid me soil my feet, lose my sweet pleasures, go naked in the winter night? Is He not a
cumbersome Christ? Are not His commandments
untimeous;[2] might He not have knocked before the
sun went down, before I went to bed? It is strange this
Christ of mine must have service betwixt midnight
and cockcrow, when all other folks are at rest."

But here is a question that is worthy of solving:
What makes this so hard to us, to go but the breadth
of the house barefooted to let Christ in? Certainly the
reasons are these.

Our light is corrupt and looks awry and with a
squinted eye upon Christ, and it looks with many
eyes to the world. Hence, when Christ knocks, it
says, first, "He cannot come here." Second: "I doubt
if it is Christ that knocks, because I wish it were not

---

1. *Quaint Sermons*, 87–91.

2. *untimeous:* at the wrong time or inconveniently late

He." Third: "I must live." Fourth: "I cannot suffer."
Fifth: "This and this will befall me if I do it." Sixth:
"If I would let Him in, then my lusts would get no
quarters with Him. My will, my affections, and He
would never give one jot. They would fly upon each
other." No, men's lusts are up where eyes should be,
and their eyes down at their feet.

Our heart and our affections hold us still in our
warm bedsheets, so that we cannot rise to let Christ
in. Yea, hardness of heart, the worst believer, and the
toughest disputer in the world carves[3] all, and when
we come to choose what to do, then we ask counsel:
"Again, what do you say, lust? What is your will and
vote? Honor, ease, etc.? Tell me. Shall I let Him in?"
And then we do not hear the other side till amen.
O, but beloved, there is a thing they call "Try all
things,"[4] and look again and fear always, so needful
here that they would pull the covering off all things
and let you see all things — whose skin is black, and
whose is white.

"How can I? How can I, Spouse?" you ask. "How
can I arise? How can I put on my coat?" I will tell
you how you can. Stir your legs and arms, and raise
your frozen fingers. It is strange to ask how a whole,
strong man who is not bound can rise out of his bed!
Stir yourself, and cast the covering and bedclothes off
and come to the floor. If men would suffer[5] their light[6]

---

3. *carves:* cuts or shapes

4. "Prove all things; hold fast that which is good" (1 Thess. 5:21).

5. *suffer:* allow

6. *light:* spiritual understanding

to play fair play[7] and think judiciously and spiritually on the world and the delights of it, which is their soft bed, they might open to Christ. Men are but sleeping on a bed of ice. It will melt with the heat of God's anger, and they and their night sheets and the bed will swim. No, men have reason to tire of this bed, both short and narrow. "Thou fool, this night thy soul shall be required of thee" (Luke 12:20). "The fashion of this world passeth away" (1 Cor. 7:31). Is not this a short bed? Fools cannot get their feet down.

---

7. *play fair play:* deal honestly

The Scottish National Covenant (1638), signed in
Greyfriars Churchyard, Edinburgh, reaffirmed the
Covenanters' commitment to Reformation principles.
Because he was banished to Aberdeen,
Rutherford was unable to sign.

12

The Rose of Sharon[1]

I am the rose of Sharon, and the lily of the valleys.
—Song of Solomon 2:1

There is not a rose outside of heaven that doesn't have a blot and thorn growing out of it, except that only Rose of Sharon, which blossoms out glory. Every leaf of the rose is a heaven and serves "for the healing of the nations"; every white and red in it is incomparable glory; every act of breathing out its smell, from everlasting to everlasting, is spotless and unmixed happiness. Christ is the outset, the master flower, the uncreated garland of heaven, the love and joy of men and angels. But the fountain-love, the fountain-delight, the fountain-joy of men and angels is more; for out of it flow all the seas, springs, rivers, and floods of love, delight, and joy. Imagine all the rain and dew, seas, fountains, and floods, since the creation, were in one cloud, and these multiplied in measures, in number to many millions of millions, and then divided in drops of showers to an answerable number of men and angels. This would be a created shower, and it would end in a certain period of time; and this huge cloud of so many rivers and

---

1. *Trial and Triumph*, 5–6.

drops would dry up and rain no more. But we cannot conceive so of Christ, for if we should imagine
millions of men and angels to have a co-eternal
dependent existence with Christ, and they were eternally in the act of "receiving grace for grace out of His
fulness," the flux and issue of grace would be eternal,
as Christ is. For Christ cannot tire or weary from eternity to be Christ; and so He must not, He cannot but
be an infinite and eternal flowing sea, to diffuse and
let out streams and floods of boundless grace. Say that
the rose were eternal; the sweet smell, the loveliness
of greenness, and color must be eternal.

Oh, what a happiness, for a soul to lose its excellency in His transcendent glory! What blessedness for
the creature, to cast in his little all in Christ's match-
less all-sufficiency! Could all the streams retire into
the fountain and first spring, they should be kept in
a more sweet and firm possession of their being in
the bosom of their first cause than in their borrowed
channels that they now move in. Our neighborhood
and retirement—to dwell forever and ever in the
fountain-blessedness, Jesus Christ, with our borrowed
goodness—is the firm and solid fruition of our eternal happy being. Christ is the sphere, the con-natural[2]
first spring and element of borrowed drops, and small
pieces of created grace. The rose is surest in being, in
beauty, on its own stalk and root. Let life and sap be
eternally in the stalk and root and the rose keep its
first union with the root, and it shall never wither,
never cast its blossom or greenness of beauty. It is

---

2. *con-natural:* belonging to as a natural accompaniment, or as a
property inherent by nature or from birth

violence for a gracious soul to be out of his stalk and root; union here is life and happiness. Therefore, the church's last prayer in canonic Scripture is for union: "Amen. Even so, come, Lord Jesus" (Rev. 22:20). It shall not be well till the Father and Christ the prime heir and all the weeping children are under one roof in the royal palace.

13

Sorrowing for an Absent Christ[1]

But Mary stood without at the sepulchre weeping.
—John 20:11

Here is a strange thing to think about. The Lord's own disciples ran away from seeking Him. One of them had said, "If all should forsake thee, yet shall I never forsake thee," and yet here is a woman more forward and more constant in seeking Christ than he is, for all his fair profession. It is not fair words and a golden profession that will take a soul to heaven and make us seek Christ rightly. We are all greatly indebted to saving grace in our seeking Christ. Here is a woman more forward in seeking Christ than all His eleven disciples are. Because she did not complete her errand that she was seeking, she could not get Christ, and therefore she will not leave, or give up, but will wait on and seek Him. A soul that is in love with Christ never completes his errand till he gets Christ Himself. You that are seeking Christ, never give over seeking till you meet with Him, for they shall at last meet with Him who lie at His door, seeking, as this woman did, who say, "I shall lie still at Thy door. Let me die there if Thou likest, and albeit it should come

---

1. *Quaint Sermons*, 75–77.

to that, I shall die, ere I go away and do not meet with Him." You may know the ardent desire of a soul after Christ can be satisfied with nothing but Himself.

We used to say the thing that one longs for is the thing he must have, and no other thing will satisfy him. A man that is hungry and longing for meat must have meat, and meat only, or else he is not satisfied, even if he gets some other thing. For a man that is in prison and longs to be free, nothing will satisfy him but liberty. Even so it is with this woman at this time; although the disciples were with her, yet nothing could comfort her till she got her lovely Lord whom she was seeking. Learn that lesson of spiritual importunity, never to give over seeking Christ when once you have begun it. Blessed are they that spend their time this way, in seeking Christ.

Mary stayed there weeping for want of Him and yet looking into the grave to see if He were there. That is a good and blessed desire and sorrow that is accompanied with doing. That is heaven's sorrow indeed that is accompanied with doing and using the means. There are two things said of Jacob (Hos. 12:4): that he wept and wrestled in prayer with God. What is the advantage of a dumb sorrow for the want of Christ? But it is a right sorrow for want of Christ that is joined with using the means to get Him. As it is in Solomon's Song 3:3, the spouse wants Christ there; she uses all means to get Him again. She goes to the watchmen and says to them, "Saw ye him whom my soul loveth?" She goes round about the city and to the daughters of Jerusalem and charges them. That proves that her sorrow is a right sorrow for the want of Christ. And you know what sort of tears the Scripture says Christ had (Heb. 5:7). He shed tears while He was in His flesh, and also He offered up prayers and strong cries to Him who was able to save Him and was heard in that He feared. And that is the grief and sorrow that will only hold the feet when men are sorrowful for want of Christ and also use the means to get Him, and not those who have only a mere wish for Christ and will not forego a morning or a night's sleep to meet with Him. That sorrow that is so is but a vain sorrow and will do no good.

14

Looking toward Zion[1]

They shall ask the way to Zion with their faces thitherward.
— Jeremiah 50:5

All the tears in the world without [repentance] are like Esau's tears, for he resolved in the days of mourning to kill his brother; they are also like Judas' tears of desperation. But these are better tears that are spoken of in Acts 20:19, where the apostle [Paul] was leaving the Ephesians to serve the Lord, with many tears and temptations. It is nothing to weep for sin for a time, but to have their faces toward Zion and asking the way to it and to weep — that is more. That is an excellent stance their face has. While they are serving the Lord and do not know where to find Him, they still have their faces toward Him. There is nothing that more easily describes the seekers of Zion and of the Lord than their right look. They do not know the way to Zion, and yet they have their face turned toward it, and so ask the way thereto.

There are three excellent looks spoken of in the Word of God: "Mine eyes fail while I wait for my God," and David's comparison: "My soul waiteth for the Lord more than they that watch for the morning:

1. *Quaint Sermons*, 175–77.

I say, more than they that watch for the morning" (Pss. 69:3; 130:6). And then to wait upon God in the day of trouble is an honest look also, and it is spoken of in Isaiah 17:7: "At that day shall a man look to his Maker, and his eyes shall have respect to the Holy One of Israel." What day is spoken of there? That day when the Lord shall visit Zion and the kirk[2] shall be left desolate, and there shall be only, as it were, gleaning grapes in it—even that which is spoken of in Isaiah 8:17: "I will wait upon the LORD, that hideth his face..., and I will look for Him."

To look to the Lord when the wind blows motes[3] and sand in your eyes is an honest look, and also to look to the kingdom of heaven and farther than time into eternity, as in Hebrews 11:9, where Abraham was content to dwell in tents and to seek no abiding city here, because he looked for a city which has foundations, whose builder and maker is God. And we should have Moses' look in the twenty-sixth verse of that chapter. He esteemed the reproach of Christ greater riches than the treasures of Egypt because he had respect to the recompense of reward. Moses looked higher than all the courtiers in Pharaoh's court did—beyond time to eternity.

And a third good look is to look to slain Christ. When the Lord shall refine the house of David and pour the spirit of supplications upon them, then they shall mourn when they look upon Him whom they have pierced. This condemns all the distorted looks that sinners in the world have, whatever they are.

---

2. *kirk:* church

3. *motes:* specks of dust

There is a look in Proverbs 21:4, a haughty look; the Lord cannot endure it. And in Proverbs 23 [vv. 26–33], the eyes behold strange women. Also, in Isaiah 56:11: "They all look to their own way, every one for his gain, from his quarter." And that look described in Ezekiel 18:15, where the house of Israel has its eyes toward the mountains and the hills. They do not look to the Lord, but to their own gods. The Lord condemns all those who do not look to Him. And it is sure that every man who in faith looks to God and Christ and heaven will follow his look. Oh that we had hearts and eyes to seek Him, and to look after Him, and to Him who is able to do this for us — to draw our hearts and eyes toward Himself, to that Lord, only wise, eternal, immortal, invisible.

Kenmure Castle was the home of Lady Jane Campbell, Viscountess of Kenmure, to whom Rutherford wrote forty-six of his letters.

15

Impression of Grace May Be Stronger Afterwards[1]

Did not our heart burn within us, while he talked with us by the way, and while he opened to us the scriptures?

—Luke 24:32

Their hearts burn while Christ speaks. These men had a cooling before, though they were believing disciples. But observe here that they feel the burning of heart not so [much] while Christ spoke to them as afterward. In verse 31, Christ vanished out of their sight and was gone, and now they take special notice, in a feeling way, of the warmness of heart they felt while He opened the Scriptures to them. The Lord preaches in a ladder reaching from earth to heaven, and Jacob sleeps and can give no judgment while he dreams. But in Genesis 28:16, when the sweet vision and preaching were ended, Jacob awakened from his sleep and said, "Surely the LORD is in this place, and I knew it not." A strong impression of the presence and glory of God sometimes comes on after the Lord is away. David desires and thirsts (he says in the wilderness of Judah), "to see thy power and thy glory, so as I have seen thee" (Ps. 63:2). The

1. *Influences*, 253–54.

enjoying of Zion and Zion's songs while the people are at home in their own land does not have such influence on their spirit as when the sanctuary's glory is removed. Then we find in Psalm 137:1: "By the rivers of Babylon, there we sat down, yea, we wept, when we remembered Zion."

While one has a fever, he may be ignorant that he has a fever, but when the cooling of health comes, then he well remembers he was sick of a fever. When there is a fever of glory on Peter, he does not know what to say, yet afterwards he makes sweet comfortable life of that glory of Christ on the mount (Mark 9:6; 2 Peter 1:16–17). When the Lord waters the sown seed and sends down new influences of grace, then it does appear what warming has been in the soul.

"Did not our hearts burn?" The godly reprove their own not knowing and not discerning of Christ in His heart-flamings of love; godly and spiritual sense challenges self-dullness.[2] "I opened to my beloved; but my beloved had withdrawn himself, and was gone" (Song 5:6). This is a fruit of Christ's withdrawing, with a challenge here of refusing to open. Ah! Why did I not open while He did lovingly stand and knock and lovingly speak, "Open to me, my sister, my dove" (Song 5:2)?

---

2. *self-dullness:* sluggish laziness of the flesh

16

━━ ◦◉◦ ━━

The Fragrance of Grace[1]

I charge you, O daughters of Jerusalem, if ye find
my beloved, that ye tell him, that I am sick of love.
What is thy beloved more than another beloved, O
thou fairest among women?
—Song of Solomon 5:8–9

"O thou fairest among women." Here is the character of the heavenly disposition of lovesickness, which is called savoriness.[2] The spouse savors of the Spirit and speaks like one sick from love, and the daughters of Jerusalem smell this savor and look on her as the fairest among women. There is a savoriness of passive grace, whereby words and behavior cast a smell, whether the children of God intend to or not, and an active savoriness, by which those who have anything of Christ can smell the savoriness of grace in others.

Now, a word regarding this savoriness, as it is (1) in the Head—in Christ—the cause and fountain, (2) in the spouse, (3) in the single members. The sweet smell of the fountain, imagine a well of rosewater, is the cause of the sweet smell that is in the streams.

---

1. *Influences*, 325–26.

2. *savoriness:* the quality of having a certain smell or aroma

1. There is dwelling in Him "all the fulness of the Godhead bodily" (Col. 2:9). "We beheld his glory, the glory as of the only begotten of the Father" (John 1:14). What a savory lump and mass of grace must the man Christ be, who is the public channel of grace! Through Him the savory waters of the sanctuary and the river of joy waters all the residents of the city of God (Ps. 46:4). Christ, God-man, is "anointed...with the oil of gladness above [His] fellows" (Ps. 45:7), without measure (John 3:34). The fullness of anointing is upon Him (Isa. 61:1; Luke 4:18). His name is as a precious ointment poured forth (Song 1:3). And the savor of the knowledge of His name in the preached gospel is sweet and savors out heaven and life eternal (2 Cor. 2:14–16). The fullness of grace in Him, out of which we all receive (John 1:16), makes Him more than savory. Natural men wonder at the gracious words that proceed out of His mouth (Luke 4:22), and enemies see some of the anointing and shining of God in Him. There was never a man who spoke like Him, never a man who did like Him. If we would come nearer to Christ by faith and love, we would smell more like Christ. Oh, what a savor His birth, His life, His precious ointments, His death, and His resurrection have! He is all savory (Song 1:3; Ps. 45:7–8), His lips "like lilies, dropping sweet smelling myrrh" (Song 5:13). His word is a sweet savor of life (2 Cor. 2:15–16). "His countenance is as Lebanon" (Song 5:15). Oh, what perfume is in His death! The smell of Lebanon is delicious.

2. There is much savoriness in the spouse, to the wonderment of many: "Who is this that cometh out of the wilderness like pillars of smoke, perfumed with myrrh and frankincense, with all powders of the merchant?" (Song 3:6). "How much better is…the smell of thine ointments than all spices!…The smell of thy garments is like the smell of Lebanon" (Song 4:10–11). Lebanon was a field where there grew odoriferous trees, roses, sweet-smelling spices, and herbs in abundance.

3. Every individual Christian has received the sweet-smelling anointing of the Spirit (1 John 2:20, 27), and "they that are after the Spirit" savor of the Spirit (Rom. 8:5).

17

The God-Man[1]

Have mercy on me, O Lord, thou son of David.
                              —Matthew 15:22

"O Lord, thou Son of David."

1. The word "Lord" holds forth Christ's Godhead; the other, "Son of David," holds forth His manhood. Here is the perfection of our Mediator—that He is the substantial covenant and Emmanuel, God with us or "God us," in a personal union; this is the substantial marriage and alliance between the two houses of heaven and earth, God and clay.

2. "He is not ashamed to call them brethren" (Heb. 2:11). And for what other reason would He take part of flesh and blood, except that He would be a child of our house (Heb. 2:14)?

3. He would be of blood like us. Not only would He come to the sick and to our bedside, but He would also lie down and be sick, taking on Himself sick clay, and be, in that condition of clay, a worm and not a man, that He might pay our debts. He would borrow a man's heart to sigh for us; man's eyes to weep for us; His spouse's body, legs, and arms to be pierced for

---

1. *Trial and Triumph*, sermon 9, 98–99.

us; our earth, our breath, our life, and soul that He might breathe out His life for us; a man's tongue and soul to pray for us. And yet He would remain God, so that He might perfume the obedience of a high priest with heaven and give to justice blood that chambered in the veins and body of God, in whom God had a personal lodging.

George Gillespie (1613–1648), Scottish commissioner
to the Westminster Assembly and Rutherford's close
friend and correspondent. The two men covenanted
to pray for each other for as long as they lived.

18

Christ the Son of David[1]

Have mercy on me, O Lord, thou son of David.
— Matthew 15:22

Consider why Christ is called the son of David, never the son of Adam or the son of Abraham. It is true that He is frequently called the Son of Man, but never when anyone prays to Him. He is reckoned, in His genealogy, as David's son, Abraham's son, the son of Adam. But "son of David" is His ordinary title when prayers are directed to Him in the days of His flesh. The reasons are these:

1. Christ had a special relation to Abraham, being His seed, but more special to David because the covenant was established in a special manner with David as king. He was the first king in whose hand God entrusted the feeding of the church, God's own flock, as God's deposit and pawn laid down.[2] The Lord established the covenant of grace with David and his son Solomon, who was to build Him a

---

1. *Trial and Triumph*, sermon 7, 73–74.

2. A *deposit*, in this case, is a contract by which a subject (the church) that belongs to one person (here, God) is entrusted to the care of another (David), to be redelivered on demand. A *pawn* is a pledge or surety. Rutherford is emphasizing the sureness of God's covenant with David.

house. God promised to David an eternal kingdom, grace, and perseverance in grace, and all of that was promised by a sure covenant, "the sure mercies of David" (Isa. 55:3; see also 2 Sam. 7:8–16; 1 Chron. 22:9–10). "Yet he hath made with me an everlasting covenant, ordered in all things, and sure: for this is all my salvation, and all my desire" (2 Sam. 23:5). "I have made a covenant with my chosen, I have sworn unto David my servant, thy seed will I establish for ever, and build up thy throne to all generations" (Ps. 89:3–4; see also vv. 21–37). Gabriel, the angel, speaks the same to Zacharias (Luke 1:32–33; see also vv. 68–69; Acts 2:30; 13:34–37). It was necessary, then, that Christ the Messiah should lineally descend from a king: Abraham was not a king; Adam was not formally a king by covenant, as David was.

2. Christ changes names with David as He never did with any other man. Christ is never called Abraham, but He is called David: "My servant David [will be] a prince among them" (Ezek. 34:23–24). "[They shall] seek the LORD their God, and David their king" (Hos. 3:5).

David took a typical throne opposed by the hearts of Jew and Gentile (Ps. 2:1–2), and so did Christ (Acts 4:25–26). David fed the people of God in the midst of many enemies (Ps. 110:1–2), and so did Christ (Acts 2:34–36). This was not so with Abraham; he was a befriended man in a strange land.

19

Numbering Our Days[1]

*So teach us to number our days, that we may apply
our hearts unto wisdom.*
                              —Psalm 90:12

All of us generally sail in the bad husbanding of time.[2]
We are dying before we know the purpose for which
we live. Imagine a master who sent his servant to a
great city with a paper containing business of great
importance. The master has allotted to his servant the
space of ten sandglasses[3] to quickly take care of the
matter. If the servant, for the space of the first nine
hours, starts drinking with his drunken companions
and goes up and down to behold all the novelties of
the city, he will break trust. Alas! Is not this world
like a great exchange? Our paper contains the business of a great kingdom up above, the honor and
glory of our Lord, our redemption through Christ, a
treaty for everlasting peace. The time of infancy and
childhood slips by, and we do not know the purpose
of our creation. Youth and adulthood are like a proud
meadow, green, fair, and delightful today, but tomor-

---

1. *Sermon Preached...Lords*, 7.

2. *husbanding of time:* To "husband time" is to cultivate or make
good use of it. Rutherford is saying that most of us waste our time.

3. *sandglasses:* hours

row it becomes hay, casting off blossoms and flowers. With one little stride we skip through our span of time. Yet we go through the exchange to buy frothy honor and rotten pleasure, and when our last hour has come, we scarcely read our Master's paper.

We barter one nothing-creature[4] for another, alas! It is a poor accounting that a natural man makes who can say nothing more at his death than "I have eaten, drunk, slept, waked, dreamed, and sinned for the space of sixty or seventy years, and that is all." Time, like a long, swift, sliding river, runs through the city from the time of creation, when God first set the clock going, to the day of Christ's second coming. This river slides through our fingers. We eat, drink, sleep, amuse ourselves, laugh, buy, sell, speak, breathe, and die in a moment. Every gasp of air is a flux of our minute's time sliding into eternity, within a few generations.... We, whose lives are only a company of night visions, shall fly away, and "our places shall know us no more." And though this should not be, the world is not eternal, being a great body made up of corruptible pieces, of little dying creatures that would be standing on nothing if God were to take the legs from them. At length God shall remove the passes of the watch, and "time shall be no more." The wheels of time shall be at a stand.... Consider the afternoon of a declining sun. Within a few hours we are plunged in the bosom and womb of eternity and cannot return.

---

4. *nothing-creature:* something insignificant

20

Wondering at Christ[1]

*And they being afraid wondered, saying one to another,
What manner of man is this! for he commandeth even
the winds and water, and they obey him.*

—Luke 8:25

We read that this is the only fruit this miracle produced in the seamen: They begin wondering because
they are astonished to see a man command the sea
and the winds.

1. The miracles of Christ and all the works of God
are so far inferior to His Word that they can teach
us nothing of the Trinity or of two natures in the one
person and of our mediator, Jesus Christ.

2. Oh how little of God do we see, especially being
void of His own light! Job says that even though God
is at our elbow, we do not know it is Him: "Behold,
I go forward, but he is not there; and backward, but I
cannot perceive him" (Job 23:8). But is this because
God was neither behind Job nor before him? No, God
goes round about us. Every man may, as it were, put
forth his hand, and touch the Almighty (Acts 17:27).
Therefore, Job adds, He is "on the left hand, where
he doth work, but I cannot behold him: he hideth

---

1. *Sermon Preached...Lords*, 63–64.

himself on the right hand, that I cannot see him" (Job 23:9). We cannot trace the footsteps of His unsearchable ways. Alas, we only amuse ourselves to see superficially the outside, as it were, the brim of divine providence. Men or angels cannot dive to the bottom of the ways of our Lord. He says Himself, "For as the heavens are higher than the earth, so are my ways higher than your ways, and my thoughts than your thoughts" (Isa. 55:9).

3. We come only as near to Christ as to go at most three or four steps towards Him.

(a) Some are convinced and wonder. They say, "This must be God," as in Luke 4:22, when Christ preaches as Christ, and like Himself, they all bear Him witness and wonder at the gracious words that proceed out of His mouth. Yet they are not a step nearer to Him. They despise Him and say, "Is not this Joseph's son?" Some know that "there hath been a prophet among them," but they are scorpions and briars and thorns and will not hear (Ezek. 2:5–6).

(b) Some are enlightened and believe for an hour (Matt. 13:20–21). Faith that lives for only an hour is a sickly, dying faith.

(c) Some are a step nearer. They have joy in Christ (Matt. 13:20), and the word of a prophet is to them "as...very lovely" (Ezek. 33:32). The gospel is sweet to many, but if they do not come nearer, they will not hear or obey.

(d) Some taste of "the good word of God" and "the powers (Gk. 'manifold powers') of the world to come" (Heb. 6:5), yet come never nearer to Christ but fall off, as if they were afraid to be converted. They do not go a fifth step further to give themselves up wholly to Jesus Christ.

If natural men wonder at the power and excellency of Christ, in that He, with a word, commands both sea and winds and they obey Him, should not Christ be to us a world's wonder? Should He not be to us altogether lovely? If it were possible to lay in the opposite scale of the balance from Christ, a world of angels, put in yet millions of worlds of angels, add to them a world of Solomons with tripled wisdom, put in all the delights of the sons of men, put in yet the flower and rose of ten thousand possible worlds' perfections, they should weigh less than He, and the balance would never [come] down.

James Guthrie (c. 1616–1661), minister at
Stirling, was executed for his opposition to giving
the king absolute authority in the church.
He corresponded with Rutherford.

21

The Signs of a New Heart[1]

A new heart also will I give you.
—Ezekiel 36:26

A new heart is the office-house of Christ, and a heart delighting in God's ways is a new heart, where the law is imprinted and engraved in the heart: "Hearken unto me, ye...people in whose heart is my law" (Isa. 51:7). "I delight to do thy will, O my God: yea, thy law is within my heart" (Ps. 40:8). It's true that for some there may be a new delight in the heart, but not a delight of the new heart (Isa. 58:2; John 5:35), for a delight in the gospel as a good thing and not as a good gospel, a delight in Christ as a prophet that feeds them and not in Christ as a Redeemer that saves them (John 6:26). This is not a new heart.

The new heart is a universal[2] heart, wholly for God as God. There is a proper blending in it when the whole "spirit and soul and body be preserved blameless" "in all holy conversation and godliness" (1 Thess. 5:23; 1 Peter 1:18; 2 Peter 3:11). Half a globe, though exquisitely planed, is not a globe, nor is half a cart wheel a cart wheel. External things may

---

1. *Covenant of Life*, 151–52.

2. *universal:* entirely for God in all areas of the heart, with no limitation

be divided. One may be a hearing professor[3] and a drunken professor, or a praising, singing professor in public, and not a praying or believing professor in private. Spiritual duties cannot be divided; half a faith, half a love, is not faith, is not love. Saving grace is an essence that consists indivisibly and cannot be parted.[4]

A new heart is fixed and established by grace. It's a new state—not a new, transient flash—but a new heart. "All that the LORD our God shall speak unto thee...we will hear," but the Lord says, "O that there were such a heart in them," but it is not in them (Deut. 5:27, 29).

"God gave [Saul] another heart" (1 Sam. 10:9). So a changed heart is not a new heart. A new spirit or a new gift in Jehu is not a new heart. It's not newness that makes the heart new, but God's new engraving (Jer. 31:33).

A heart kept with all keeping is a new heart (Prov. 4:23). Both the words[5] denote exact diligence in keeping, as watchmen and shepherds tend their charges at all times (Ps. 119:129). Some drag their hearts to pray and hear, but not until the Sabbath or during a storm of conscience, and in some company they will speak about the heart, but not at other times and in other company.

---

3. *professor:* one who makes open profession of religious faith

4. According to Aristotle and Scholastic thought, spiritual substances such as the soul or abstract virtues were indivisible essences that could not be broken up into constituent parts.

5. The Hebrew of Proverbs 4:23 can be rendered "above all keeping, keep thine heart." "Keep" (*natsar*) and "diligence" (*mishmar*) both mean "to guard."

(1) The heart is new where the affections are all faith (as it were) and all sanctified, reason and zeal is a lump of angry reason, fear is a mass of shining reverence, and love is solely soul-sickness and pure adherence to God. The instinct of faith is wholly towards God, as the last and only end. (2) The heart is new when the affections are equivocally or, at least at the secondhand, set upon the creature, but as nothing can be seen but what either is color or affected with color, so nothing is fixedly sought after but God.[6] Only He is feared and served (Deut. 10:20; Matt. 4:10). Only He is desired and loved (Deut. 10:12; Ps. 73:25; Song 3:2–3). The soul is sick with love for only Christ (Song 2:5; 5:8). Only He is trusted (Ps. 62:5; Jer. 17:5, 7). Nothing is all good and all desirable but God, and God in Christ (Matt. 19:17; Song 5:16). The shadow of the sun in the fountain is not the real sun. The stirrings of the pulse of the affections towards the shadowed good of the creature should be lent, and, like the beating of the pulse of a dying man, with a godly contradiction, loving and not loving, joying and not joying, mourning and not mourning (1 Cor. 7:29–30).

---

6. In the same way as nothing in this world can be seen without light and distinguished from other things without color, so the renewed soul comes to see all things in the light of God Himself and in connection with Him.

22

The Prince of Life Lays Down His Own Life[1]

Jesus cried with a loud voice, and gave up the ghost.
—Mark 15:37

O Life! Wouldst Thou bear that blessed body company no longer? O Life of Life! Wouldst Thou be taken death's prisoner? Oh to see that blessed head fall to the one side! Oh to see Life wanting life! To see Life lying dead! To see that blessed mouth silent! To see that fair corpse rolled in linen and laid in a tomb! Oh to see sweet Jesus, that blessed body, in Joseph's arms! Come hither, come hither, believers, and see a sight that you never saw the like of! Oh, what would the disciples say but, "We are beguiled men! We thought that He should have restored the kingdom to Israel, and now He is gone away, and now He is dead, the One that raised Lazarus from the grave." Oh, angels would think, "Our Master is dead." There must have been much scarcity of life in the world (one might say), for Him to have died for want of it!

The whole guard about Christ might say, "Oh, what evil has He done?" O sun! Why would you

1. *An Exhortation at a Communion, to a Scots Congregation in London* (Glasgow, 1804), 12–13.

not lend Him light? He never angered you, but gave you light! O floods, O rivers, O running streams! What has angered you at your Creator, that you would not send your Lord a drink? O bread! Why are you gall to Him? O drink! Why are you vinegar to Him? O worldly pomp and glory, what ails[2] you at Him—that He is so ashamed? O life, where are you going? Why do you leave the Lord of Life? O joys! Why would you not cheer Him? O disciples, why did you leave and forsake Him? O Father, what ails Thee at Thy dear and only Son? O what evil way went these feet, that they are pierced? What evil have these hands done that they are pierced? O what evil and what vanity did these eyes behold, that death has closed them? O what sin has that fair face done, that it is spat on? O what did these hands steal, that they are bound? O what evil has that blessed Head done, that it is crowned with thorns?

---

2. *ails:* to be troubled by or at someone

23

Christ's Dove[1]

O my dove, that art in the clefts of the rock, in the
secret places of the stairs, let me see thy countenance,
let me hear thy voice; for sweet is thy voice, and thy
countenance is comely.
        —Song of Solomon 2:14

[Christ] calls [the church] His "dove." He regrets
nothing that He said. He abides by His word. He calls
her His love, His fair one, His undefiled. He avows[2]
it. He abides by it. [He says,] "You are even My
dove"; yet He is not flattering her. If you are Christ's,
He will give you all your styles[3] of honor; He will
speak much good of you, both behind your back and
before your face.

She is termed Christ's dove:

1. Because the dove is a fearful bird, and soon scared.
"They shall tremble...as a dove out of the land of
Assyria" (Hos. 11:11). Anything, the smallest noise
or din that can be, frightens and chases these timorous
birds in their dove-house, into Christ. It is a happy
rain that chases Christ's doves in to Himself. For all

---

1. *Communion Sermons*, 248–51.

2. *avows:* promises with a vow

3. *styles:* titles

the Devil's wit, he is soon beguiled; the storm that arises against the ship where Christ and His disciples are makes them awaken and pray.

2. The dove is a mournful bird; the doves of Christ are also mourning and in tears. "They that escape of them shall escape, and shall be on the mountains like doves of the valleys, all of them mourning, every one for his iniquity" (Ezek. 7:16). If you are God's doves, you will have many sorrowful days in the world. There are bloody wars between the kirk[4] and the world. Keep the dove from the nest, and she mourns without; keep the kirk from Christ, and she will break her heart.

3. She is not a vengeful bird; she has no armor against the ravens and vultures other than her wings to flee away. God's children's best armor when they are wronged is by faith in prayer to mount up to God. They must be like Christ. He went out of the world with many wrongs [done to Him], and they are not yet revenged. His blood is keeping to the last court-day. Christ sits with many wrongs in heaven; He has not gotten amends from those that spat in His face. Many times the kirk and her Husband, Christ, will be wronged here, although it is between them (Song 5). She thrusts Him to the door and lets Him lodge all night in the rainy fields.

4. And then fourthly, the kirk is like a dove mourning without a marrow;[5] for that fowl cannot want a marrow. If you are God's doves, woe will you be when

---

4. *kirk:* church

5. *marrow:* spouse; match

your marrow, Christ, flies away. She swoons, and her heart flies out of her when Christ flies away.

5. The dove is an innocent, harmless bird; she cannot offend. So is the kirk; the meek spouse of Christ will not marrow with a malicious house.

6. The dove is a silly, weak, tender fowl, and if it is compared to the rest of the birds, it is valued only at a tenth of flying fowls. Surely God's kirk in herself is but a weak bird and tender woman, compared in Revelation 12 to a woman who has just delivered a child, and there is little between her death and her life if she is not carefully attended. A Christian is a tender thing, a jewel in the hand of Christ. If He lets us fall, we are soon broken in pieces. We should pray that Christ will handle us softly and not let us be tempted above our strength. The kirk is called a crippled woman that goes only upon her one side (Mic. 4:6). So surely we had need to come out of the wilderness leaning on our Beloved (Song 8:5).

7. And for their number, they are only a handful (Isa. 6:13). The tithe or remnant, God's part, is but a tenth, and the Devil has all the stock; often God has one, and the devil nine. We have great need to labor to be of God's tenth.

Alexander Henderson (1583–1646), a Scottish
theologian, one of the Scottish commissioners
to the Westminster Assembly, and one of
Rutherford's correspondents.

24

The Ways and Dealings of the King of Kings to a Soul[1]

My beloved spake, and said unto me...
— Song of Solomon 2:10

Now the church relates the words of her Beloved calling upon her; see how many ways the Lord shows Himself to His church: (1) He speaks to her ear. (2) He runs and leaps before her eye. (3) He stands behind the wall. (4) He looks out at the window to her. (5) He ends as He began and speaks to her ear. This lets us see there are some happy times, wherein Christ presses Himself upon His children and fills ears, eyes, tongues, hands, hearts—fills all—with Christ. The soul of the child of God has certain feast days; it is with the child of God as it is with the Jordan [River] when all the banks are full. Sometimes the soul will be full of Christ, so that it is full from bank to brae.[2] See how Christ fills the apostle in 1 John 1:1, 3: "That which was from the beginning, which we have heard, which we have seen with our eyes, which we have looked upon, and our hands have handled, of the Word of life;...that which we

---

1. *Communion Sermons*, 321–22.

2. *brae:* the steep or sloping bank of a river

have seen and heard declare we unto you." Behold, the apostle is going round about Christ and filling himself with Christ, like hungry men at a feast. They hear Him, they see Him, they look upon Him, and eye Him, and even more, they handle Him with their hands. Oh these are glorious times when the child of God gets a great feast of Christ! And if He fills us here while we are [away] from home and are such narrow-hearted vessels that God must enlarge us, how full shall we be of God when we shall see Him as He is (Ps. 119:32)! "My soul shall be satisfied as with marrow and fatness" (Ps. 63:5). "Eat, O friends; drink, yea, drink abundantly, O beloved" (Song 5:1). When any of these glorious times come, we may not think that Christ will [go] away again. What should we then do? Even as Joseph did; he caused his brethren to leave a pledge to assure him that they would return again. So you must cause Jesus to leave His seal and His ring and some footsteps of His grace and take instruments in the hand of the Spirit, that He will return.

You see in the church a sweet and commendable virtue in these words. She sets down the very progress of all the ways and dealings of the King of Kings to her soul. In all His ways she sees what Christ is doing; when He is far off, she knows Him, she sees Him running and leaping, she sees Him behind the wall, looking out at the windows, and through the lattice. She hears Him hand speaking.[3] She writes up His very words. We see the child of God marks the ebbings and the flowings, the comings and goings of

---

3. *hand speaking:* whispering

the Spirit of God, and sees Christ in all His footsteps. When Christ comes at the dead hour of the night, she hears His knocks through her sleep and knows His voice. He can put in His hand and open the bar of her conscience to come in. She knows what He is doing. She feels the smell that drops from His fingertips. What breeds experience of Christ? A daily walking with Him. You know of the courtiers that are around the king's person day and night; they can write a chronicle of the king's life and can tell how many miles he rides in the day. So says David, "My eyes are ever towards the Lord."

25

Christ's Joy[1]

…who for the joy that was set before him…
—Hebrews 12:2

1. The joy before Him was the contentment He would have in His new bride—the joy that He had won through hell and gotten by His errand. His heart would have been sad and heavy to have missed us. He was glad of the hire[2] His Father had promised Him. It is natural for a man to rejoice when he gets the fruit of his labors, and there is thanksgiving and joy in heaven for the conversion of sinners. And He gives thanks far more when they are redeemed fully. In the midst of the congregation, He sings praise to God His Father for the children He had given Him, but He will do so even more when He has ended all and got the goods in His hand that He bought so dearly (Heb. 2:12). He will then sing for joy, and when Christ sings for your redemption and gives thanks, you have far more cause to sing than He.

2. The joy set before Him was the glory to be manifested in Him, for which He prays (John 17:5), which "He had with [the Father] before the world

---

1. *Communion Sermons*, 107–108.

2. *hire:* payment, reward

was"—that joy that His Father will welcome Him with and (to speak with reverence) clap[3] His head for His pains. As He rejoiced from all eternity with His Father (Prov. 8:31) and was His Father's delight, so now He shall rejoice with His Father, He and He together in redeemed mankind. And the manhood[4] with all His members and the angels (for they rejoice at the conversion of sinners) shall rejoice with Him to see His body fulfilled and to have them all under His wings.

Consider the sadness Jesus had and the tears He shed in the days of His flesh; but His Father dried and wiped the blood and sweat off His face and set Him in a place where He would no longer shed tears and die. So do as Jesus did. And why? Because there was never a man who endured his longsome[5] race but the one who had a sight of heaven. See wherefore Abraham dwelt in tents, and Moses (Heb. 11) "[chose] rather to suffer affliction with the people of God, than to enjoy the pleasures of sin" (Heb. 11:25). He saw a sight that not everyone can see. You know that a man who has been seven years away from his wife and children comes home again, and, as he sees the smoke of his own house, his heart rises a foot higher than it was before. Would you run? Get a sight of the city. Get Christ's prospect[6] to see the joy set before you. Get the earnest[7] of the inheritance,

---

3. *clap:* pat fondly

4. *manhood:* human nature

5. *longsome:* tiresomely long

6. *prospect:* view

7. *earnest:* token of what is to come

and you will never rue[8] the bargain. Whoever has a mind for heaven runs a while in blind zeal until he sweats and then grows lame, like a horse that is badly taken care of after hard riding; so are those who never saw heaven afar off by faith. But a sight of the gold makes the runner spring and run. Oh what wrought this joy that was set before Him! It made Him endure the cross; His Father laid the cross on His back, and He carried it thirty-three years and never gave it a shake to put it off. Oh, what crosses! Never man was handled as He was; for some are under some crosses and free of others. When Satan and men struck Job, the Lord blessed him and upheld him. But on Jesus, all at once fell God, man, devils, law, justice, sin, and the curse! You cannot tell me what comfort Christ had when He cried, "My God, my God!" That was a sore thraw[9] for His back. Oh the fire was hot then! But when Christ was in His prison, in this dark night, there was a hole to let Him see day. He had His eye by faith upon the hope of the joy of the fair day before Him. He got a foul black day, all clouds of darkness about Him, but He said within Himself, "I will get my fair day when all this ill weather is away."

---

8. *rue:* regret

9. *thraw:* a twist or wrench of a part of the body

26

Mysteries in Christ[1]

> *And he had a name written, that no man knew, but he himself.*
> —Revelation 19:12

Oh what a nameless king is this! What? Is Christ unbaptized that He lacks a name? Is there no man who knows His name? "What is his name, and what is his son's name, if thou canst tell?" (Prov. 30:4). "He was taken from prison and from judgment: and who shall declare his generation?' (Isa. 53:8). Here is a strange thing! The angel says, "Thou shalt call his name Jesus." Nay, but His name is Himself and His nature, and so He is an infinite God. None knows infinite Christ but Himself. Aye, surely Christ is an unknown person; though each one has Christ Jesus in his mouth, yet he does not know what he is saying.

There are three mysteries in Christ we cannot perfectly know or understand in this life:

1. The infinite wisdom, mercy, goodness, love, and grace in Christ, which the angels delight to look into and wonder. Come near Christ, and you will never see the bottom of Him. You have seen mercy, great mercy; there is yet more behind. One has seen much

1. *Communion Sermons*, 17–18.·

of Him, another more; the angels that are sharp in sight have yet seen more; nay, but there is infinite more behind. You will as soon take the sea in the hollow of your hand and bind the wind in your cloak as you will take Him up. You must even stand still here and wonder and cry out, "Oh great Jesus, who will or can fathom Thee out?"

2. Oh what a depth is in the work of Christ's incarnation! God and dust married together! How [can it be that] blood remains in a personal union with God! How [can it be that] the finite Manhood subsists in His infinite personality! And how [can it be that] the Godhead in the second person, and not in the first or third, assumed our nature, and yet there is but one Godhead in all the three! How [can it be that] the Godhead stood under the Manhood that was stricken, and the Godhead as a back-friend[2] held Him up, and yet the Godhead suffered not! How [can it be that] Jesus-man died and Jesus-God lived and remained in death God and man!

3. The third mystery is this: what a name Jesus has gotten by His rising from the dead, and how the Manhood is advanced. Christ kens[3] all these full well; He can read His own name. You will speak of learning to measure the earth, number the stars, and learning their motion—that is deep knowledge; but God help you to come hither and see this unknown name, *Jesus,* and find it out if you can. I know you cannot.

---

2. *back-friend:* a friend to help

3. *kens:* knows

Where will you set Christ? Where will you get a seat, a throne, a chair to Him? He cannot be set too high; nay, if there were ten thousand times ten thousand heavens, and each above another, and Christ were set in the highest of them all, yet He would be too low.

Oh, let us long for glory, that place where we will read His name clearly and will see Christ face to face. Oh, strange that we do not long to be in heaven, to see this comely glorious one (if I may so speak), a darling indeed, and to play God's bairns[4] in heaven! We will then come and look into the ark; for the curtain will be drawn by, and we will see our fill of Christ there.

---

4. *bairns:* children

John Livingstone (1603–1672), a Scottish minister
who was exiled from Scotland for refusing to take the
oath of allegiance as dictated to him, was
one of Rutherford's correspondents.

27

The Danger of Seeking Material Things[1]

Father, give me the portion of goods that falleth to me.
—Luke 15:12

You heard the substance of the young man's [the prodigal son's] prayer: "Father, give me the portion of goods that falleth to me." There is no word of his asking that his father would bless him or that he seeks his father's favor and goodwill to the purpose that he is upon, but rather he says, "Give me the portion of goods that falleth to me." The meaning is, "Give me my own will to follow my way with something of this life"; there is the sinner's heart-wish morning and evening. All that the sinner seeks here is something divided from God, that he may get some created perishing thing out of his Father's hand. That is all that a sinner can seek who is left and forsaken of God—the world, the glory thereof, or something to satisfy the lawless desire of his heart and lusts. That is all the divinity the natural man has.

In a word, it is only this life that the natural man seeks, even that which our Lord reproves, "Verily, verily, I say unto you, Ye seek me, not because ye saw

1. *Quaint Sermons*, 219–21.

the miracles, but because ye did eat of the loaves, and were filled." He tells them what to seek and what not to seek: "Labour not for the meat which perisheth, but for that meat which endureth unto everlasting life, which the Son of man shall give unto you" (John 6:26–27). That is only reason from our darkened judgments that do not see things rightly, and from this, the sinner is always at something that he believes to be heaven and happiness, when indeed it is not so, for there is nothing in the creature can do so.

But is there nothing at all in the creature that is good or can make a man good and happy? Yes, all the creatures of God in their own kind are good. But when we make any of the creatures an idol and make them a god, when we trust in the creature and place our happiness and heaven in them, then all the creatures are nothing else but vanity and vexation of spirit. When we do so, then there is nothing good at all that is under the sun. When the creature is in any way divided from God, then it is not good. Whatever you would rest upon without God or beside Him is evil. The creature as a creature is good; but the creature as an idol and a god is evil.

May we not, then, seek after the creature? Yes, but if you seek it right, it must be sought in God, the Creator. Seek ourselves in God, and we shall certainly find ourselves there. Seek yourselves and seek the creature for God, and then you shall find God and the creature and yourselves. But if you seek God outside of God, and seek the creature outside of God, then you are seeking fire under you. And all natural men, thus, are seeking fire under them. They seek their good things outside of God, and so they never get satisfaction to the soul. They seek a good thing that is like themselves. As it is in Psalm 4:6, "Many...say, Who will shew us any good?" But the next verse tells us what the natural man's good things are—to have his corn, wine, and oil abound. His thought is how his house may be built up, and yet leave enough to his children behind him, as it is in Psalm 49:11. And when they have gotten what their hearts are after, they are not a whit more happy, but rather further from happiness than before.

28

Testing Ourselves[1]

*Examine yourselves, whether ye be in the faith; prove
your own selves. Know ye not your own selves, how
that Jesus Christ is in you, except ye be reprobates?*
— 2 Corinthians 13:5

You doubt, from 2 Corinthians 13:5, whether you
are in Christ or not? And so then, whether you are a
reprobate or not? I answer two things to the doubt.
First, you owe charity to all men, but most of all to
lovely and loving Jesus and some also to yourself,
especially to your renewed self, because your new self
is not yours but another Lord's, even the work of His
own Spirit. Therefore, to slander His work is to wrong
Him. Love thinks no evil; if you love grace, think not
ill of grace in yourself. The great Advocate pleads
hard for you; be upon the Advocate's side, O poor,
feared client[2] of Christ! He pleads for you, whereof
your letter (though too, too full of jealousy) is a proof.

For if you were not His, your thoughts (which, I
hope, are but the suggestions of His Spirit, who only
brings the matter into debate to make it sure to you)
would not be such nor so serious as these, "Am I

---

1. *Letters*, no. 293, 588.

2. *client:* follower, or dependent

His?" or "Whose am I?" Second, dare you forswear your Owner and say in cold blood, "I am not His"? What nature or corruption says in the first place in you, I regard not. Your thoughts of yourself, when sin and guiltiness round you in the ear and when you have a sight of your deserving, are apocryphal and not Scripture, I hope. I charge you by the mercies of God, be not that cruel to grace and the new birth as to cast water on your own coal by misbelief.

You may put a difference between you and reprobates, if you have these marks.[3]

1. If you prize Christ and His truth so as you will sell all and buy Him, and suffer for it.

2. If the love of Christ keeps you from sinning, more than the law or fear of hell.

3. If you are humble and deny your own will, wit, credit, ease, honor, the world, and the vanity and glory of it.

4. Your profession must not be barren and void of good works.

5. You must in all things aim at God's honor; you must eat, drink, sleep, buy, sell, sit, stand, speak, pray, read, and hear the Word, with a heart purpose that God may be honored.

6. You must show yourself an enemy to sin and reprove the works of darkness, such as drunkenness, swearing, and lying, albeit the company should hate you for so doing.

---

3. *Letters*, no. 172, 324.

7. Keep in mind the truth of God that you heard me teach, and have nothing to do with the corruptions and new guises entered into the house of God.

8. Make conscience of your calling in covenants and in buying and selling.

9. Acquaint yourself with daily praying; commit all your ways and actions to God by prayer, supplication, and thanksgiving; and count not much of being mocked; for Christ Jesus was mocked before you.

Persuade yourself of this: "This is the way of peace and comfort for which I now suffer. I dare go to death and into eternity with it, though men may possibly see another way."

29

Covenant Love between God and His People[1]

I will say, It is my people: and they shall say, The LORD is my God.
—Zechariah 13:9

There is (if we may so speak) a shaking of hands on both sides. There God claims kindness to His people, and they claim kindness to Him; He takes hold of them, and they cleave to Him; He loves them, and they love Him. Kindness between God and His people never stands on one side; it is on both sides. However, God must begin. Love is not an herb that grows with the root uppermost and the top down: it does not grow up, but comes down from God, and the beams of it spring up to Him again.

See this meeting: the church says, "Draw me" (Song 1:4). She speaks to Christ to draw her; then says Christ, "Rise up, my love, my fair one, and come away" (Song 2:10). He seeks her, and she seeks Him. She says, "Tell me, O thou whom my soul loveth, where thou feedest" (Song 1:7). I will be where Thou dwellest; I will be where Thou art. Christ seeks you in the sacrament; you seek Him again, and though the Devil should say the contrary, there shall be a meet-

1. *Communion Sermons*, 44–45.

ing. She says, "Saw ye him whom my soul loveth?" (Song 3:3). He says, "Come with me from Lebanon" (Song 4:8). He calls her. She says, "We will remember thy love more than wine" (Song 1:4). He says, "How much better is thy love than wine!" (Song 4:10). He calls her, "my love, my fair one" (Song 2:10). She says that He is "white and ruddy, the chiefest among ten thousand" (Song 5:10).

Let His love get a meeting. He fought through death and hell to find you; seek Him through all troubles. He bought you dear;[2] you say, "O that I could buy Him, and give all that I have or could do for Him." There is not any blessed marriage otherwise. Do you not love Christ clearly? Would you not suffer and die for Him, as He suffered and died for you? It is not marriage-love if it is not so; it is but feigned love. Now Christ is holding forth His love to you this day. Will you not accept the offer, and will you return nothing again? I like not that kindness[3] when there is no taking and giving, no borrowing and lending betwixt Christ and you. May the Lord Jehovah persuade you to embrace the offer and flee into lovely Christ Jesus, the glorious Prince of renown, and to Him be praise forever and ever. Amen.

---

2. *bought you dear:* at an expensive price

3. *kindness:* relationship

William Guthrie (1620–1665) was a Scottish Puritan
minister and author who was brought to Christ
by Rutherford's ministry at St. Andrews;
he was one of Rutherford's correspondents.

30

Christ Cannot Be Hid[1]

*And from thence [Christ] arose, and went into the
borders of Tyre and Sidon, and entered into an
house, and would have no man know it: but he
could not be hid. For a certain woman, whose young
daughter had an unclean spirit, heard of him, and
came and fell at his feet.*
— Mark 7:24–25

"But he could not be hid."

1. Christ desired not to be hid from this woman; He
was seeking her, and yet He flies from her. Christ, in
this, is such a flier as would gladly have a pursuer.

2. Faith finds Christ out when He is hid. "Verily thou
art a God that hidest thyself" (Isa. 45:15). But faith
sees God under His mask and through the cloud,
and, therefore, faith adds, "O God of Israel, the
Savior! Thou hidest Thyself, O God, from Israel, but
Israel finds Thee." "Israel shall be saved in the LORD
with an everlasting salvation" (Isa. 45:17). God casts
a cloud of anger about Himself; He makes darkness
His pavilion and will not look out. Yet Job sees God
and finds Him out many hundred miles: "Yet in my
flesh shall I see God" (Job 19:26).

---

1. *Trial and Triumph*, sermon 2.

3. Reason, sense, nay, angels, seeing Christ between two thieves dying and going out of this world, bleeding to death, naked, forsaken of friend and lover, may wonder and say, "Oh Lord, what art Thou doing here?" Yet the faith of the thief found him there, as a king who had the keys of Paradise; and he said in faith, "Lord, remember me when thou comest into thy kingdom" (Luke 23:42).

4. Faith sees Him as a witness and a record in heaven, like Job (Job 16:19), even when God cleaves his reins asunder and pours out his gall upon the ground (Job 16:13). Believe then that Christ frowns that He may kiss; that He cuts that He may cure; that He makes the living believer's grave before his eyes and has no mind to bury him alive. He breathes the smoke and the heat of the furnace of hell on the soul, when peace, grace, and heaven are in His heart. He breaks the hollow of Jacob's thigh so that he must go crippled all his days, and it is His purpose to bless him. Whereas we should walk by faith, we walk much, even in our spiritual walk, by feeling and sense; we have these errors in our faith. We do not make the word of promise the rule of our faith, but only God's dispensation.

31

Hearing of the Lord Jesus Christ[1]

A certain woman, whose young daughter had an unclean spirit, heard of him, and came and fell at his feet.
— Mark 7:24–25

What had she heard?

1. That Jesus was the Son of God, the Messiah of Israel, and could, and was willing, to heal her daughter. Two things are here observable: (1) Hearing of Christ drew her to Christ. (2) It is good to border[2] with Christ, and to be near at hand to Him. There is a necessity that we hear of Christ before we come to Him. This is God's way: "Faith cometh by hearing" (Rom. 10:17). Christ is not in us from the womb; faith is not a flower that grows out of such a sour and cold ground as nature; it is a stem and a birth of heaven.

2. None can come to Christ, except they hear a good report of Him. How shall they believe in Him of whom they have not heard? Those who come aright to Christ must have noble, high, long, deep, and broad thoughts of Jesus and know the gospel. Now, what is the gospel? Nothing but a good report of

---

1. *Trial and Triumph*, sermon 5.

2. *border:* lie on the border with; touch along a boundary

Christ. You must hear a gospel-report of Christ before you come to Him; ill-principled thoughts of Christ keep many from Him. "[Strangers] shall hear of thy great name, and of thy strong hand" (1 Kings 8:42). Christ was to be heard by the deaf Gentiles: "In that day shall the deaf hear the words of the book" (Isa. 29:18). We hear, and we hear not, because the Lord does not waken the ear, morning by morning, that we may hear as the learned. Many hear, but they have not the learned ear or the ear of such as have heard and learned of the Father. Many hear of Christ, a voice, and no more but a voice; they know not that prophecy, "Thine ears shall hear a word behind thee, saying, This is the way, walk ye in it" (Isa. 30:21). There is another voice in our hearing; men do not hear, that they may hear. "Hear, ye deaf; and look, ye blind, that ye may see" (Isa. 42:18); that is, hear that you may hear, see that you may see. The Lord gives grace that He may give grace, and we are to receive grace that we may receive grace; grace is the only reward of grace.

3. We hear and we hear not; we see, but we have no reflex act upon our seeing. Many open their ears to Christ, but they hear not; they want a spiritual faculty of observing. "Seeing many things, but thou observest not; opening the ears, but he heareth not" (Isa. 42:20).

Many put Christ in an ear without a bottom or in an ear with a hole in its bottom; we hear of Christ, but we are as leaking and running out vessels (Heb. 2:1). "Who among you will give ear to this? who will hearken and hear for the time to come?" (Isa. 42:23).

Physicians give their three causes of deafness. (1) When there is carnosity[3] on the eardrum. This is extrinsic: the world is another lover, and the care of it; and that hinders hearing. (2) When the organ of hearing is hurt and distempered, as a lame hand that cannot apprehend: now, when there are false fancies and principles contrary to the gospel in the heart, the ear cannot hear. (3) When there is abundance of humors in the brain, and they raise a noise and tumult in the drum and hinder sounds to be heard. When pride and principles of sensuality and vain pleasures make a noise within so that neither Christ knocking nor His voice without can be heard, men are deaf.

---

3. *carnosity:* a fleshy growth

32

Return to Your First Husband[1]

Therefore, behold, I will hedge up thy way with thorns, and make a wall, that she shall not find her paths. And she shall follow after her lovers, but she shall not overtake them.
—Hosea 2:6–7

Whatever you love besides Jesus, your husband, is an adulterous lover. Now it is God's special blessing to Judah that He will not let her find her paths in following her strange lovers. "Therefore, behold, I will hedge up thy way with thorns, and make a wall, that she shall not find her paths. And she shall follow after her lovers, but she shall not overtake them" (Hos. 2:6–7). O thrice happy Judah, when God builds a double stone wall betwixt her and the fire of hell! The world and the things of the world, Madam, is the lover you naturally affect[2] beside your own husband, Christ. The hedge of thorns and the wall that God builds in your way, to hinder you from this lover, is the thorny hedge of daily grief, loss of children, weakness of body, iniquity of the time, uncertainty of estate, lack of worldly comfort, fear of God's anger for old unrepented-of sins. What do you lose if God twists and plaits the hedge

---

1. *Letters*, no. 4, 40–41.

2. *affect:* have affection for

thicker daily? God be blessed, the Lord will not let you find your paths. Return to your first husband.

Do not weary, neither think that death walks towards you with a slow pace. You must be riper before you are shaken. Your days are no longer than Job's, that were "swifter than a post...[and] passed away as the swift ships: as the eagle that hasteth to the prey" (Job 9:25–26). There is less sand in your glass now than there was yesternight. This span of ever-fleeting time will soon be ended. But the greater is the mercy of God, the more years you get to consider upon what terms and upon what conditions you cast your soul in the huge gulf of never-ending eternity. The Lord has told you what you should be doing till He comes. "Wait and hasten," says Peter, "for the coming of our Lord."

All that is here is night, in respect to ignorance and daily ensuing troubles, one always making way for another, as the ninth wave of the sea to the tenth; therefore sigh and long for the dawning of that morning and the breaking of that day of the coming of the Son of Man, when the shadows shall flee away. Persuade yourself the King is coming; read His letter sent before Him: "Behold, I come quickly" (Rev. 3:11). Wait with the wearied night-watch for the breaking of the eastern sky, and think that ye have not a morrow. As the wise father said, who, being invited against to-morrow to dine with his friend, answered, "Those many days I have had no morrow at all." I am loath to weary you. Show yourself a Christian by suffering without murmuring, for which sin 14,700 were slain (Num. 16:49). In patience possess your soul. They lose nothing who gain Christ.

The Grassmarket, or market square,
of seventeenth-century Edinburgh, with
Edinburgh Castle towering over it.

33

Zion's Lament[1]

Zion said, The LORD hath forsaken me, and my Lord hath forgotten me. Can a woman forget her sucking child, that she should not have compassion on the son of her womb? yea, they may forget, yet will I not forget thee. Behold, I have graven thee upon the palms of my hands; thy walls are continually before me.

—Isaiah 49:14–16

Know that I am in great heaviness for the pitiful case of our Lord's kirk. I hear that the reason why Dr. Burton[2] is committed to prison is his writing and preaching against the Arminians. I therefore entreat the aid of your prayers for myself and the Lord's captives of hope and for Zion. The Lord has let and daily lets me see clearly how deep furrows Arminianism and the followers of it draw upon the back of God's Israel (but our Lord cut the cords of the wicked!). "Zion said, The LORD hath forsaken me, and my Lord hath forgotten me" (Isa. 49:14). "[Zion] weepeth sore in the night, and her tears are on her cheeks: among all her lovers she hath none to com-

---

1. *Letters*, no. 17, 64–65.

2. Dr. Burton was Henry Burton, an able divine of the Church of England who wrote several vigorous pieces against popery and against Montague's *Appello Cæsarem*.

fort her: all her friends have dealt treacherously with her, they are become her enemies" (Lam 1:2). "Thy silver is become dross, thy wine mixed with water" (Isa. 1:22). "How is the gold become dim! How is the most fine gold changed! The stones of the sanctuary are poured out in the top of every street. The precious sons of Zion, comparable to fine gold, how are they esteemed as earthen pitchers, the work of the hands of the potter!" (Lam. 4:1–2).

It is time now for the Lord's secret ones, who favor the dust of Zion, to cry, "How long, Lord?" and to go up to their watchtower, and to stay there, and not to come down until the vision speak; for it shall speak (Hab. 2:3). In the meantime, the just shall live by faith. Let us wait on and not weary. I have not a thread to hang upon and rest but this one: "Can a woman forget her sucking child, that she should not have compassion on the son of her womb? yea, they may forget, yet will I not forget thee. Behold, I have graven thee upon the palms of my hands; thy walls are continually before me" (Isa. 49:15–16). For all outward helps do fail; it is time therefore for us to hang ourselves, as our Lord's vessels, upon the nail that is fastened in a sure place. We would make stakes of our own fastening, but they will break. Our Lord will have Zion on His own nail.

Edom is busy within us and Babel without us against the handful of Jacob's seed. It were best that we were upon Christ's side of it, for His enemies will get the stalks to keep,[3] as the proverb is. Our greatest difficulty will be to win upon the rock now, when the

---

3. Christ's enemies will get only withered stalks to keep.

wind and waves of persecution are so lofty and proud. Let sweet Jesus take us by the hand. Neither must we think that it will be otherwise; for it is told to the souls under the altar that "their fellowservants...should be killed as they were" (Rev. 6:11). Surely, it cannot be long till the day. Nay, hear Him say, "Behold, I come, My dear bride; think not long. I shall be at you at once. I hear you and am coming." Amen. Even so, come, Lord Jesus, come quickly; for the prisoners of hope are looking out at the prison windows to see if they can behold the King's ambassador coming with the King's warrant and the keys. I do not write to you by guess now, because I have a warrant to say unto you that the garments of Christ's spouse must be once again dyed in blood, as long ago her Husband's were. But our Father sees His bleeding Son.

34

Life Which Cannot Be Lost[1]

Your life is hid with Christ in God.
—Colossians 3:3

"Your life is hid with Christ in God," and therefore you cannot be robbed of it (Col. 3:3). Our Lord handles us as fathers do their young children; they lay up jewels in a place, above the reach of the short arm of bairns,[2] else bairns would put up their hands and take them down and lose them soon. Our Lord has done this with our spiritual life. Jesus Christ is the high coffer in which our Lord has hid our life; we children are not able to reach up our arm so high as to take down that life and lose it; it is in our Christ's hand. O long, long may Jesus be Lord Keeper of our life! Happy are they that can, with the apostle, lay their soul in pawn[3] in the hand of Jesus, for He is able to keep that which is committed in pawn to Him against that day (2 Tim. 1:12).

Then, Madam, so long as this life is not hurt, all other troubles are but touches in the heel. I trust you will soon be cured. You know, Madam, kings have

---

1. *Letters*, no. 27, 86–87.

2. *bairns:* children

3. *pawn:* pledge, surety

some servants in their court that do not receive present wages in their hand, but live upon their hopes. The King of Kings also has servants in His court that for the present get little or nothing but the heavy cross of Christ, troubles without and terrors within; but they live upon hope, and when it comes to the parting of the inheritance, they remain in the house as heirs. It is better to be so than to get present payment and a portion in this life, an inheritance in this world (God forgive me, that I should honor it with the name of an inheritance, it is rather a farm-room![4]), and then in the end to be cast out of God's house with this word, "You have received your consolation; you will get no more." Alas! What do they get? The rich glutton's heaven (Luke 16:25). Oh, but our Lord makes it a silly[5] heaven! "He fared well," says our Lord, "and delicately every day." Oh, no more? A silly heaven! Truly no more, except that he was clothed in purple, and that is all.

I persuade myself, Madam, you have joy when you think that your Lord has dealt more graciously with your soul. You have gotten little in this life—it is true indeed. You have then the more to crave— yea, you have all to crave—for, except some tastings of the first fruits and some kisses of His mouth whom your soul loves, you get no more. But I cannot tell you what is to come. Yet I may speak as our Lord does of it. The foundation of the city is pure gold, clear as crystal. The twelve ports are set with pre-

---

4. *farm-room:* a rented room

5. *silly:* poor, pitiful

cious stones. If orchards and rivers commend[6] a soil upon earth, there is a paradise there where grows the tree of life that bears twelve manners of fruits every month, which is seven score and four[7] harvests in the year. And there is a pure river of water of life, proceeding out of the throne of God and of the Lamb. And the city has no need of the light of the sun or moon or of a candle, for the Lord God Almighty and the Lamb is the light thereof. Madam, believe and hope for this, till you see and enjoy. Jesus is saying in the gospel, "Come and see." And He is come down in the chariot of truth, which He rides through the world to conquer men's souls (Ps. 45:4), and is now in the world saying, "Who will go with Me? Will you go? My Father will make you welcome and give you houseroom;[8] for in My Father's house are many mansions." Madam, consent to go with Him.

---

6. *commend:* to set off to advantage

7. *seven score and four:* 144

8. *houseroom:* lodging

35

Christ's Goodwill for the Suffering Church[1]

...the good will of him that dwelt in the bush.
—Deuteronomy 33:16

I entreat you charge your soul to return to rest and to glorify your dearest Lord in believing, and know that for the goodwill of Him that dwells in the bush, the burning kirk[2] shall not be consumed to ashes, but "blessing [shall] come upon the head of Joseph, and upon the top of the head of him that was separated from his brethren" (Deut. 33:16). And are not the saints separate from their brethren and sold and hated? For "the archers have sorely grieved [Joseph], and shot at him, and hated him: but his bow abode in strength, and the arms of his hands were made strong by the hands of the mighty God of Jacob" (Gen. 49:23–24). From Him is the Shepherd and the Stone of Israel. The Stone of Israel shall not be broken in pieces; it is hammered upon by the children of this world, and we shall live and not die. Our Lord has done all this to see if we will believe and not give up,

---

1. *Letters*, no. 38, 102–103.

2. *kirk:* church

and I am persuaded you must of necessity stick by your work. The eye of Christ has been upon all this business, and He takes good heed to who is for Him and who is against Him. Let us do our part, as we would be approved of Christ. The Son of God is near to His enemies.

If they were not deaf, they would hear the din[3] of His feet. He will come with a start upon His weeping bairns[4] and take them on His knee and lay their head in His bosom and dry their watery eyes. And this day is fast coming. Yet a little time, and the vision will speak; it will not tarry (Hab. 2:3). These questions betwixt us and our adversaries will all be decided in yonder day, when the Son of God shall come, and redd[5] all pleas; and it will be seen whether we or they have been for Christ and who has been pleading for Baal. It is not known what we are now; but when our life shall appear in glory, then we shall see who laughs fastest that day. Therefore, we must possess our souls in patience and go into our chamber and rest, till the indignation is past.

We shall not weep long when our Lord shall take us up, in the day that He gathers His jewels. "They that feared the LORD spake often one to another, and the LORD hearkened, and heard it, and a book of remembrance was written before him for them that feared the LORD, and that thought upon his name" (Mal. 3:16). I shall never be of another belief but that our Lord is heating a furnace for the enemies of

---

3. *din:* noise

4. *bairns:* children

5. *redd:* settle

His kirk in Scotland. It is true the spouse of Christ has played the harlot and has left her first Husband, and the enemies think they do not offend, for we have sinned against the Lord; but they shall get the devil to their thanks. The rod shall be cast into the fire so that we may sing as in the days of our youth. My dear friend, therefore, lay down your head upon Christ's breast. Weep not; the Lion of the tribe of Judah will arise. The sun is gone down upon the prophets, and our gold is become dim, and the Lord feeds His people with waters of gall and wormwood; yet Christ stands behind the wall. His bowels[6] are moved for Scotland. He waits, as Isaiah says, that He may show mercy. If we could go home and take our brethren with us, weeping with our face toward Zion, asking the way thitherward, He would bring back our captivity. We may not think that God has no care of His honor while men tread it under their feet. He will clothe Himself with vengeance, as with a cloak, and appear against our enemies for our deliverance. You were never yet beguiled,[7] and God will not now begin with you. Wrestle still with the angel of the covenant, and you shall get the blessing. Fight! He delights to be overcome by wrestling.

---

6. *bowels:* pity, compassion, heart

7. *beguiled:* disappointed

Rutherford wrote this letter to Sir James Stewart, Lord Provost of Edinburgh, on the occasion of his election to Professor of Divinity at the College of Edinburgh. A transcription can be found in *Letters*, no. 325.

36

The False Glory of the World[1]

The fashion of this world passeth away.
—1 Corinthians 7:31

I bless our Lord, through Christ, who has brought you home again to your own country from that place[2] where you have seen with your eyes that which our Lord's truth taught you before—to wit, that worldly glory is nothing but a vapor, a shadow, the foam of the water, or something less and lighter, even nothing; and that our Lord has not without cause said in His Word, "The countenance," or fashion, "of this world passeth away" (1 Cor. 7:31)—in which place our Lord compares it to an image in a looking glass, for it is the looking glass of Adam's sons. Some come to the glass and see in it the picture of *honor*—and only a picture indeed, for true honor is to be great in the sight of God. Others see in it the shadow of *riches*—and only a shadow indeed, for durable riches stand as one of the maids of Wisdom upon her left hand (Prov. 3:16). A third sort see in it the face of painted *pleasures*, and the beholders will not believe that the image they see in this glass is not a living

---

1. *Letters*, no. 42, 108–110.

2. Edinburgh

man until the Lord comes and breaks the glass in pieces and removes the face, and then, like Pharaoh awakened, they say, "And behold it was a dream."

I know your Ladyship thinks you have little in common with this world, for the favorable aspect of any of these three painted faces, and blessed be our Lord that it is so. The better for you, Madam; they are not worthy to be wooers, to suit in marriage your soul, that look to no higher match than to be married upon painted clay. Know, therefore, Madam, the place whither our Lord Jesus comes to woo a bride. It is even in the furnace. For if you are one of Zion's daughters (which I ever put beyond all question, since I first had occasion to see in your Ladyship such pregnant evidences of the grace of God), the Lord, who has His fire in Zion and His furnace in Jerusalem (Isa. 31:9), is purifying you in the furnace. And therefore be content to live in it and every day to be adding and sewing to a pasment[3] to your wedding garment, that you may be at last decorated and trimmed as a bride for Christ, a bride of His own busking,[4] beautified in the hidden man of the heart. "[Forgetting]...thy father's house; so shall the king greatly desire thy beauty" (Ps. 45:10–11).

If your Ladyship is not changed (as I hope you are not), I believe you esteem yourself to be of those whom God has tried these many years and refined as silver. But, Madam, I will show your Ladyship a privilege that others want and you have, in this case. Such as are in prosperity and are fatted with earthly

---

3. *pasment:* strips of lace sewed on a dress for decoration

4. *busking:* adorning

joys and increased with children and friends, though the Word of God is indeed written to such for their instruction, yet to you who are in trouble (spare me, Madam, to say this), from whom the Lord hath taken many children and whom He hath exercised otherwise, there are some chapters, some particular promises in the Word of God, made in a most special manner, which should never have been yours, as they now are, if you had your portion in this life as others. And, therefore, all the comforts, promises, and mercies God offers to the afflicted are as so many love letters written to you. Take them to you, Madam, and claim your right, and do not be robbed. It is no small comfort that God has written some Scriptures to you that He has not written to others. You seem in this to be envied rather than pitied; and you are indeed in this, like people of another world and those that are above the ordinary rank of mankind, whom our King and Lord, our Bridegroom Jesus, in His love letter to His well-beloved spouse, has named beside all the rest. He has written comforts and His hearty commendations in Isaiah 54:4–5 and Psalm 147:2–3 to you. Read these and the like, and think your God is like a friend that sends a letter to a whole house and family but speaks in His letter to some by name that are dearest to Him in the house.

You are, then, Madam, of the dearest friends of the Bridegroom. If it were lawful, I would envy you, that God honored you so above many of His dear children. Therefore, Madam, your part is, in this case (seeing God takes nothing from you but that which He is to supply with His own presence), to desire your Lord to know His own room and take it even upon Him to come in, in the room of dead children. "Jehovah, know Thy own place and take it to Thee," is all you have to say.

Madam, I persuade myself that this world is to you a strange inn, and you are like a traveller who has his bundle upon his back and his staff in his hand and his feet upon the door-threshold. Go forward, honorable and elect lady, in the strength of your Lord (let the world bide at home and keep the house), with your face toward Him who longs more for a sight of you than you can do for Him. Before long, He will see us. I hope to see you laugh as cheerfully after noon as you have mourned before noon. The hand of the Lord, the hand of the Lord be with you in your journey. What have you to do here? This is not your mountain of rest. Arise, then, and set your foot up the mountain; go up out of the wilderness, leaning upon the shoulder of your Beloved (Song 8:5). If you knew the welcome that waits for you when you come home, you would hasten your pace; for you shall see your Lord put up His own holy hand to your face and wipe all tears from your eyes; and I believe, then you shall have some joy of heart.

———⊳•◦(•)•◦•⊲———

37

I Have Overcome the World[1]

In the world ye shall have tribulation: but be of good cheer; I have overcome the world.
—John 16:33

If you were not strangers here, the dogs of the world would not bark at you. You may see all windings and turnings that are in your way to heaven in God's Word, for He will not lead you to the kingdom at the nearest, but you must go through "honour and dishonour, by evil report and good report: as deceivers, and yet true; as unknown, and yet well known; as dying, and, behold, we live; as chastened, and not killed; as sorrowful, yet always rejoicing" (2 Cor. 6:8–10). The world is one of the enemies that we have to fight with, but it is a vanquished and overcome enemy and like a beaten and forlorn soldier, for our Jesus has taken the armor from it. Let me then speak to you in His words: "Be of good courage," says the Captain of our salvation, "for I have overcome the world" (John 16:33).

You shall neither be free of the scourge of the tongue nor of disgraces (even if it were buffetings and spittings upon the face, as was our Savior's case) if you follow Jesus Christ. I beseech you in the

---

1. *Letters*, no. 54, 127.

bowels of our Lord Jesus; keep a good conscience, as I trust you do. You live not upon men's opinion; gold may be gold and have the king's stamp upon it when it is trampled upon by men. Happy are you if, when the world tramples upon you in your credit and good name, yet you are the Lord's gold, stamped with the King of heaven's image and sealed by the Spirit unto the day of your redemption. Pray for the spirit of love, for love "beareth all things, believeth all things, hopeth all things, endureth all things" (1 Cor. 13:7).

38

The Hope of Glory[1]

Christ in you, the hope of glory.
—Colossians 1:27

I would but desire to stand at the outer side of the
gates of the New Jerusalem and look through a hole
of the door and see Christ's face. A borrowed vision
in this life would be my borrowed and begun heaven,
until the long, long-looked-for-day dawn. It is not
for nothing that it is said, "Christ in you, the hope
of glory" (Col. 1:27). I will be content of no pawn[2]
of heaven but Christ Himself; for Christ, possessed
by faith here, is young heaven and glory in the bud.
If I had that pawn, I would endure horning[3] and
hell both, ere I gave it again. All that we have here
is scarce the picture of glory. Should not we young
bairns[4] long and look for the expiring of our minor-
ity? It were good to be daily begging propines[5] and
love-gifts and the Bridegroom's favors, and, if we

---

1. *Letters*, no. 130, 256.

2. *pawn:* pledge

3. *horning:* A legal demand for payment of a debt under threat of
imprisonment and being proclaimed rebels. It used to be proclaimed
by the sound of a horn in the marketplace.

4. *bairns:* children

5. *propines:* presents

can do no more, to seek crumbs and hungry dinners of Christ's love, to keep the taste of heaven in our mouth until suppertime. I know it is far after noon, and the marriage-supper of the Lamb will be soon; the table is covered already. O Well-beloved, run—run fast! O fair day, when will you dawn! O shadows, flee away!

I think hope and love, woven through other,[6] make our absence from Christ spiritual torment. It is a pain to wait; but hope that "maketh not ashamed" swallows up that pain (Rom. 5:5). It is not unkindness that keeps Christ and us so long apart. What can I say to Christ's love? I think more than I can say. To consider that my Lord Jesus may take the air [7] (if I may so speak) and go abroad, yet He will be confined and keep the prison with me! But in all this sweet communion with Him, what am I to be thanked for? I am but a sufferer. Whether I will or not, He will be kind to me. He so bears His love in on me that it is as if He had defied my guiltiness that would make Him unkind. Here I die with wondering that justice does not hinder love; for there are none in hell, nor out of hell, more unworthy of Christ's love.

---

6. *woven through other:* blended into each other so that they cannot be separated

7. *take the air:* take a walk

John Maitland, Duke of Lauderdale (1616–1682),
was a Scottish politician who was a commissioner to the
Westminster Assembly. Later, under King Charles II,
Lauderdale led the brutal and bloody persecution of the
Covenanters, with which his name is now
infamously associated.

39

All Things for Good[1]

And we know that all things work together for good to them that love God.
　　　　　　　　　　　　　—Romans 8:28

I would not have you to think it strange that your journey to New England has gotten such a dash.[2] It indeed has made my heart heavy; yet I know it is no dumb providence, but a speaking one, whereby our Lord speaks His mind to you, though for the present you do not well understand what He says. However it is, He who sits upon the floods has shown you His marvelous kindness in the great depths. I know that your loss is great and your hope is gone far against you, but I entreat you, sir, expound aright our Lord's laying all hindrances in the way. I persuade myself that your heart aims at the footsteps of the flock, to feed beside the shepherds' tents and to dwell beside Him whom your soul loves, and that it is your desire to remain in the wilderness, where the woman is kept from the dragon (Rev. 12:14). And as this is your desire, remember that a poor prisoner of Christ said

---

1. *Letters*, no. 161, 298–300.

2. This correspondent, John Stuart, because of the oppressive measures of the prelates, intended to emigrate to New England. He had been forced to give up his plans. A "dash" is an affliction or discouragement.

to you that that miscarried journey is with child to
you of mercy and consolation and shall bring forth a
fair birth on which the Lord will attend. Wait on; "He
that believeth shall not make haste" (Isa. 28:16).

I hope that you have been asking what the Lord
means and what further may be His will in reference
to your return. My dear brother, let God make of
you what He will; He will end all with consolation
and will make glory out of your sufferings. Would
you wish better work? This water was in your way
to heaven and written in your Lord's book; you were
obligated to cross it and, therefore, kiss His wise and
unerring providence. Do not let the censures of men,
who see only the outside of things—and scarce well
that, abate your courage and rejoicing in the Lord.
Although your faith sees only the black side of providence, it has a better side, and God will let you see it.
Learn to believe Christ better than His strokes, Himself and His promises better than His glooms.

Dashes and disappointments are not canonical
Scripture; fighting for the Promised Land seemed to
cry to God's promise, "Thou liest." If our Lord were
to ride upon a straw, His horse would neither stumble
nor fall. "And we know that all things work together
for good to them that love God" (Rom. 8:28); therefore, shipwreck, losses, etc., work together for the
good of them that love God. Hence, I infer that
losses, disappointments, ill-tongues, loss of friends,
houses, or country are God's workmen, set on work
to work out good to you, out of everything that
befalls you. Do not let the Lord's dealing seem harsh,
rough, or unfatherly because it is unpleasant. When
the Lord's blessed will blows across your desires, it is

best, in humility, to strike sail to Him and to be willing to be led any way our Lord pleases. It is a point of denial of yourself to be as if you had not a will but had made a free disposition of it to God and had sold it over to Him. And to make use of His will for your own is both true holiness, and your ease and peace. You do not know what the Lord is working out of this, but you shall know it hereafter.

And what I write to you, I write to your wife. I feel compassion for her case but entreat her not to fear or faint. This journey is a part of her wilderness to heaven and the Promised Land, and there are fewer miles behind. It is nearer the dawning of the day to her than when she went out of Scotland. I should be glad to hear that you and she have comfort and courage in the Lord.

40

Christ and His People
in the Wilderness[1]

*Therefore, behold, I will allure her, and bring her
into the wilderness, and speak comfortably unto her.*
—Hosea 2:14

I rejoice that He is come and has chosen you in the
furnace; it was even there where you and He set
tryst.[2] That is an old gate[3] of Christ's: He keeps the
good old fashion with you that was in Hosea's days:
"Therefore, behold, I will allure her, and bring her
into the wilderness, and speak [to her heart]" (Hos.
2:14). There was no talking to her heart while He
and she were in the fair and flourishing city and at
ease, but out in the cold, hungry, waste wilderness,
He allured her. He whispered news into her ear there
and said, "Thou art Mine." What would you think
of such a bode?[4] You may soon do worse than say,
"Lord, hold all; Lord Jesus, a bargain it is. It shall not
go back on my side."

---

1. *Letters*, no. 186, 363–65.

2. *tryst:* a meeting at a certain place and time

3. *gate:* way, manner of doing

4. *bode:* offer with view to a bargain

You have gotten a great advantage in the way of heaven, that you have started to the gate in the morning. Like a fool, as I was, I suffered my sun to be high in the heaven and near afternoon before ever I took the gate by the end. I pray you, now keep the advantage you have. My heart, be not lazy; set quickly up the brae[5] on hands and feet, as if the last pickle[6] of sand were running out of your glass and death were coming to turn the glass. And be very careful to take heed to your feet in that slippery and dangerous way of youth that you are walking in. The devil and temptations now have the advantage of the brae of you and are upon your wand-hand and your working-hand.[7] Dry timber will soon take fire. Be covetous and greedy of the grace of God, and beware that it be not a holiness which comes only from the cross; for too many are that way disposed. "When He slew them, then they sought him, and they returned and enquired early after God.... Nevertheless they did flatter him with their mouth, and they lied unto him with their tongues" (Ps. 78:34, 36). It is part of our hypocrisy to give God fair, white words when He has us in His grips (if I may speak so) and to flatter Him till He win[8] to the fair fields again. Try well green[9] godliness, and examine what it is that you love in Christ. If you love only Christ's sunny side and would

---

5. *brae:* hill

6. *pickle:* small grain

7. The *wand-hand* is the hand that holds the rod, or whip, and the hand that guides the horse is the *working hand.*

8. *win:* reaches, attains to

9. *green:* to long after

have only summer weather and a landgate,[10] not a sea-way, to heaven, your profession will play you a slip, and the winter-well will go dry again in summer.

Make no sport nor bairn's[11] play of Christ; but labor for a sound and lively sight of sin, that you may judge yourself an undone man, a damned slave of hell and of sin, one dying in your own blood, except Christ come and rue[12] for you and take you up. And, therefore, make sure and fast work of conversion. Cast the earth deep. And down, down with the old work, the building of confusion that was there before; and let Christ lay new work and make a new creation within you. Look to see if Christ's rain goes down to the root of your withered plants and if His love wound your heart until it bleeds with sorrow for sin and if you can pant and fall aswoon and be like to die for that lovely one, Jesus. I know that Christ will not be hid where He is; grace will ever speak for itself and be fruitful in well-doing. The sanctified cross is a fruitful tree; it brings forth many apples.

---

10. *landgate:* land way

11. *bairn's:* children's

12. *rue:* be sorry

41

Altogether Lovely[1]

He is altogether lovely.
—Song of Solomon 5:16

Christ is a well of life; but who knows how deep it is to the bottom? This soul of ours has love and cannot but love some fair one. And oh, what a fair One, what an only One, what an excellent, lovely, ravishing One is Jesus! Put the beauty of ten thousand thousand worlds of paradises, like the garden of Eden, in one. Put all trees, all flowers, all smells, all colors, all tastes, all joys, all sweetness, all loveliness, in one. Oh, what a fair and excellent thing would that be! And yet it would be less to that fair and dearest Well-beloved, Christ, than one drop of rain to the whole seas, rivers, lakes, and fountains of ten thousand earths.

Oh, but Christ is heaven's and earth's wonder! What marvel that His bride says, "He is altogether lovely!" (Song 5:16). Oh that black souls will not come and fetch all their love to this fair One! Oh, if I could invite and persuade thousands and ten thousand times ten thousand of Adam's sons to flock about my Lord Jesus and to come and take their fill of love! Oh, pity for evermore, that there should be

---

1. *Letters*, no. 226, 446–48.

such a one as Christ Jesus, so boundless, so bottomless, and so incomparable in infinite excellency and
sweetness, and so few to take Him! Oh, oh, you poor,
dry, and dead souls, why will you not come hither
with your toom[2] vessels and your empty souls to this
huge and fair and deep and sweet well of life, and fill
all your toom vessels? Oh that Christ should be so
large in sweetness and worth and we so narrow, so
pinched, so ebb, and so void of all happiness.

And yet men will not take Him! They lose their
love miserably, those who will not bestow it upon
this lovely One. Alas! These five thousand years,
Adam's fools, his waster heirs (Prov. 18:9), have
been wasting and lavishing out their love and their
affections upon black lovers and black harlots, upon
bits of dead creatures and broken idols, upon this and
that feckless[3] creature, and have not brought their
love and their heart to Jesus. Oh, pity, that Fairness
has so few lovers! Oh, woe, woe to the fools of this
world who run by Christ to other lovers! Oh, misery,
misery, misery, that comeliness can scarce get three
or four hearts in a town or country! Oh that there is
so much spoken and so much written and so much
thought of creature vanity and so little spoken, so
little written, and so little thought of my great and
incomprehensible and never-enough-wondered-at
Lord Jesus! Why should I not curse this forlorn[4] and
wretched world that suffers my Lord Jesus to lie by

2. *toom:* entirely empty

3. *feckless:* worthless

4. *forlorn:* prodigal

Himself? O damned souls! O miskenning[5] world! O
blind, O beggarly and poor souls! O bewitched fools!
What ails you at Christ that you run so from Him? I
dare not challenge providence, that there are so few
buyers and so little sale for such an excellent one as
Christ. (O the depth and O the height of my Lord's
ways, that pass finding out!)

But oh, if men would once be wise and not fall
so in love with their own hell as to pass by Christ
and misken Him! But let us come near and fill ourselves with Christ, and let His friends drink and be
drunk and satisfy our hollow and deep desires with
Jesus. Oh, come all and drink at this living well;
come, drink and live forevermore; come, drink, and
welcome! "Welcome," says our fairest Bridegroom.
No man gets Christ with ill will; no man comes and
is not welcome. No man comes and is sorry for his
voyage; all men speak well of Christ who have been
at Him. Men and angels who know Him will say
more than I can do and think more of Him than they
can say. Oh, if I were misted[6] and bewildered in my
Lord's love! Oh, if I were fettered and chained to it!
Oh, sweet pain, to be pained for a sight of Him! Oh,
living death; oh, good death; oh, lovely death, to die
for love of Jesus! Oh that I should have a sore heart
and a pained soul for the want of this and that idol!
Woe, woe to the mistakings of my miscarrying heart,
that gapes and cries for creatures and is not pained
and cut and tortured and in sorrow for the want of a
soul's-fill of the love of Christ! Oh that Thou wouldst

---

5. *miskenning:* disregarding, ignoring

6. *misted:* lost like one in a mist

come near, my Beloved! O my fairest One, why dost Thou stand afar! Come hither, that I may be satiated with Thy excellent love. Oh, for a union! Oh for a fellowship with Jesus! Oh that I could buy with a price that lovely One, even suppose that hell's torments for a while were the price! I cannot believe but Christ will be sorry for His pained lovers and come and ease sick hearts who sigh and swoon for want of Christ.

Archibald Johnston, Lord Warriston (1611–1663),
Scottish judge and statesman who attended
the Westminster Assembly.

42

Suffering with Christ[1]

...the fellowship of [Christ's] sufferings...
　　　　　　　　　—Philippians 3:10

Madam, subscribe to the Almighty's will; put your hand to the pen, and let the cross of your Lord Jesus have your submissive and resolute amen. If you ask and try whose this cross is, I dare say that it is not all your own. The best half of it is Christ's. Then your cross is no bastard, but is lawfully begotten; it sprang not out of the dust (Job 5:6). If Christ and you are halvers[2] of this suffering and He says, "Half mine," what should ail you? And I am sure that I am here right upon the style of the Word of God: "the fellowship of [Christ's] sufferings" (Phil. 3:10); "that which is behind of the afflictions of Christ" (Col. 1:24); "the reproach of Christ" (Heb. 11:26). It would be to shift[3] the comforts of God to say, "Christ never had such a cross as mine. He never had a dead child, and so this is not His cross; neither can He, in that meaning, be the owner of this cross." But I hope that Christ, when

---

1. *Letters*, no. 287, 565–66.

2. *halvers:* partners, each owning a half

3. *shift:* evade

He married you, married you and all the crosses and woe[4] hearts that follow you.

And the word makes no exception: "In *all* their affliction he was afflicted" (Isa. 63:9, emphasis added). Then Christ bore the first stroke of this cross; it rebounded off Him upon you, and you get it secondhand. You and He are halvers in it. And I shall believe, for my part, that He desires to distill heaven out of this loss and all others the like; for wisdom devised it, and love laid it on, and Christ owns it as His own and puts your shoulder beneath only a piece of it. Take it with joy as no bastard cross, but as a visitation of God, well-born; and spend the rest of your appointed time, till your change come, in the work of believing. And let faith, that never yet lied to you, speak for God's part of it, "He will not, He does not, make you a sea or a whale-fish, so that He can keep you in ward"[5] (Job 7:12). It may be that you do not think many of the children of God are in such a hard case as yourself. But what would you think of some who would exchange afflictions and give you to the boot?[6] But I know that yours must be your own alone, and Christ's together.

---

4. *woe:* sorrowful

5. *ward:* a place of confinement

6. *boot:* an instrument of torture that would crush the bones of the victim's lower leg and foot

43

Christian Directions[1]

1. That during the hours of the day, shorter and longer periods of time for the Word and prayer should be given to God, not sparing the twelfth hour, or midday; howbeit it should then be the shorter time.

2. In the midst of worldly employments, there should be some thoughts of sin, death, judgment, and eternity, with at least a word or two of ejaculatory prayer to God.[2]

3. To beware of wandering of heart in private prayer.

4. Not to grudge if you come from prayer without sense of joy. Downcasting,[3] a sense of guiltiness, and hunger are often best for us.

5. That the Lord's Day, from morning to night, be spent always either in private or public worship.

---

1. *Letters*, no. 159, 293.

2. The eighteenth-century Scottish divine James Fisher gives us one of the best definitions of ejaculatory prayer: "It is a secret and sudden lifting up of the soul's desires to God, upon any emergency that may occur in providence" (*The Westminster Assembly's Shorter Catechism Explained* [1753; repr., Philadelphia: Presbyterian Board of Publication, n.d.], 217).

3. *downcasting:* depression

6. That words be observed, wandering and idle thoughts be avoided, sudden anger and desire of revenge, even of such as persecute the truth, be guarded against; for we often mix our zeal with our wildfire.

7. That known, discovered, and revealed sins that are against the conscience be avoided, as most dangerous preparatives to hardness of heart.

8. That in dealing with men, faith and truth in covenants and trafficking[4] be regarded, that we deal with all men in sincerity; that conscience be made of idle and lying words; and that our carriage be such, as that they who see it may speak honorably of our sweet Master and profession.

---

4. *trafficking:* dealings, transactions

King Charles II of England (1630–1685)
banned Rutherford's *Lex Rex* and had Rutherford
arrested and tried for treason.

Monument to Rutherford on
Boreland Hill in Anwoth.

Reading Rutherford

Biographies of Rutherford

Coffey, John. *Politics, Religion and the British Revolutions: The Mind of Samuel Rutherford.* Cambridge: Cambridge University Press, 1997. This is the definitive intellectual and scholarly biography of Rutherford's life and work with particular focus given to *Lex, Rex* in its context.

Rendell, Kingsley G. *Samuel Rutherford: A New Biography of the Man and His Ministry.* Fearn: Christian Focus Publications, 2003. This work was originally a master's thesis. It is not as comprehensive as Coffey's book, but it is well-researched and perhaps more accessible to the general reader. Rendell helpfully focuses on Rutherford's ability as an apologist and propagandist.

Thomson, Andrew. *The Life of Samuel Rutherford.* Glasgow: Free Presbyterian Publications, 1988. This is a small but relatively full biography in which one of the leading evangelicals in the Church of Scotland in the early nineteenth century shows appreciation for Rutherford.

Rutherford's Works

Barnes, Stanley, comp. *An Inspirational Treasury on Samuel Rutherford.* Belfast: Ambassador Productions, 2001. An anthology that includes Alexander

Whyte's appreciation of Rutherford, a selection of Rutherford's sayings, excerpts from his letters, and four of his better known sermons.

Fourteen Communion Sermons. Edinburgh: Blue Banner Productions, 1986. These sermons by Rutherford are in a volume originally edited by Andrew Bonar.

Letters of Samuel Rutherford: A Selection. Edinburgh: Banner of Truth, 1996. An abridged edition that contains sixty-nine of the letters.

Letters of Samuel Rutherford: With a Sketch of His Life and Biographical Notes of His Correspondents by Andrew A. Bonar. Edinburgh: Banner of Truth Trust, 1984. This definitive edition includes 365 letters, a glossary, and brief biographical introduction. Portage Publications has made an electronic edition available that can be downloaded free of charge from http://www.portagepub.com/products/caa/index.html

Lex, Rex, or the Law and the Prince: A Dispute for the Just Prerogative of King and People. Berryville, Va.: Hess Publications, 1998, or Harrisonburg, Va.: Sprinkle Publications, 1982. *Lex, Rex* means "The law is king." The subtitle gives the historical background: "containing the reasons and causes of the most necessary defensive wars of the Kingdom of Scotland, and of their Expedition for the aid and help of their dear brethren of England; in which their innocency is asserted." Rutherford pursues his argument through forty-four questions, or chapters, for limited monarchy as opposed to absolute or divine right monarchy. Most notably, he argues for the right to resist monarchs when they violate the law.

The Loveliness of Christ. Edinburgh: Banner of Truth, 2007. This attractively produced gift book contains short extracts and quotations of Rutherford's thoughts from his letters.

The Power of Faith and Prayer. Stornoway: Reformation Press, 1991. First published in 1713 as *The Power and Prevalency of Prayer*, this is an incomplete series of sermons by Rutherford on Matthew 9:27–31. There is a brief preface by the publishers and selections from the preface to the 1713 edition. Modern equivalents of obsolete words in the text are supplied by the publishers.

Quaint Sermons of Samuel Rutherford. Morgan, Pa.: Soli Deo Gloria, 2003. This book contains eighteen sermons first published in 1885 from a manuscript volume of Rutherford's sermons transcribed in shorthand by one of his hearers.

Rutherford's Catechism, or, The Sum of Christian Religion. Edinburgh: Blue Banner Productions, 1998. A new edition of Rutherford's catechism together with a fragment of a catechism by Robert Blair.

Trial and Triumph of Faith. Edinburgh: Banner of Truth, 2001. These twenty-seven sermons focus on Christ's dealings with the Syro-Phoenician, including frequent refutations of antinomianism.

Popular

Cook, Faith. *Grace in Winter.* Edinburgh: Banner of Truth, 1996. The author transforms some of Rutherford's letters into poetry and provides historical background on the correspondents.

————. *Samuel Rutherford and His Friends*. Edinburgh: Banner of Truth, 1996. A collection of short biographies of some of Rutherford's correspondents together with extracts from the letters. This is a popular but interesting and quite well-researched book.

Internet Resources

The website www.samuelrutherford.org.uk seeks to provide a comprehensive information source in relation to Rutherford's works and Rutherford studies with links to online resources.